DIGITAL
PORTFOLIOS
in the Classroom

DIGITAL
PORTFOLIOS
in the Classroom

Showcasing and Assessing Student Work

Matt Renwick

Alexandria, Virginia USA

1703 N. Beauregard St. • Alexandria, VA 22311-1714 USA
Phone: 800-933-2723 or 703-578-9600 • Fax: 703-575-5400
Website: www.ascd.org • E-mail: member@ascd.org
Author guidelines: www.ascd.org/write

Deborah S. Delisle, *Executive Director;* Robert D. Clouse, *Managing Director, Digital Content & Publications;* Stefani Roth, *Publisher;* Genny Ostertag, *Director, Content Acquisitions;* Allison Scott, *Acquisitions Editor;* Julie Houtz, *Director, Book Editing & Production;* Jamie Greene, *Associate Editor;* Thomas Lytle, *Senior Graphic Designer;* Mike Kalyan, *Director, Production Services;* Circle Graphics, *Typesetter;* Kelly Marshall, *Senior Production Specialist*

All web links in this book are correct as of the publication date below but may have become inactive or otherwise modified since that time. If you notice a deactivated or changed link, please e-mail books@ascd.org with the words "Link Update" in the subject line. In your message, please specify the web link, the book title, and the page number on which the link appears.

PAPERBACK ISBN: 978-1-4166-2464-6   ASCD product #117005   n8/17
PDF E-BOOK ISBN: 978-1-4166-2465-3; see Books in Print for other formats.

Quantity discounts are available: e-mail programteam@ascd.org or call 800-933-2723, ext. 5773, or 703-575-5773. For desk copies, go to www.ascd.org/deskcopy.

Library of Congress Cataloging-in-Publication Data

Names: Renwick, Matt, author.
Title: Digital portfolios in the classroom : showcasing and assessing student work / Matt Renwick.
Description: Alexandria, Virginia : ASCD, [2017] | Includes bibliographical references and index.
Identifiers: LCCN 2017026437 (print) | LCCN 2017029820 (ebook) | ISBN 9781416624653 (PDF) | ISBN 9781416624646 (pbk.)
Subjects: LCSH: Electronic portfolios in education.
Classification: LCC LB1029.P67 (ebook) | LCC LB1029.P67 R43 2017 (print) | DDC 371.39—dc23
LC record available at https://lccn.loc.gov/2017026437

---

26 25 24 23 22 21 20 19 18 17   1 2 3 4 5 6 7 8 9 10 11 12

DIGITAL
PORTFOLIOS
in the Classroom

Introduction

Assessment is messy. I'm not referring to the standardized forms of assessment that are typical in schools today. The tools and results they produce are clean but show little more than a score or basic indicator of a student's current ability. The messiness I'm referring to includes the day-to-day, in-the-moment assessment that reveals information to inform teaching and learning. These assessments offer a more complete picture of a student's current abilities and dispositions. Indeed, assessment of this nature can reveal the student behind the symbols and numbers and tell his or her whole story.

Teachers know what this latter type of assessment looks and feels like, yet it can be hard to describe and capture—hence the messiness. What assessment resembles in this context might be a frustrated look or a sense of excitement while working on a new project. I've found that when I ask teachers what they most enjoy about working in education, their responses usually reflect these types of moments:

- "When their eyes light up when they finally get something."
- "When that light bulb turns on."

- "When students can see how they've progressed over the course of the school year."

The purpose of this book is to provide a guide for teachers to capture, organize, analyze, and take action on the more discrete and qualitative pieces of information in the classroom. An abundance of 21st century tools now available offer opportunities for students to represent their learning that is more in line with their understanding. Digital portfolios offer one such opportunity. The documentation of audio, video, images, text, and creative content should be held in the same regard as their quantitative counterparts (Figure 0.1). It's the goal of this book to help educators use this information to drive their instruction. Teaching becomes more rewarding when we can experience the true impact of our instruction in ways that better illustrate the whole child.

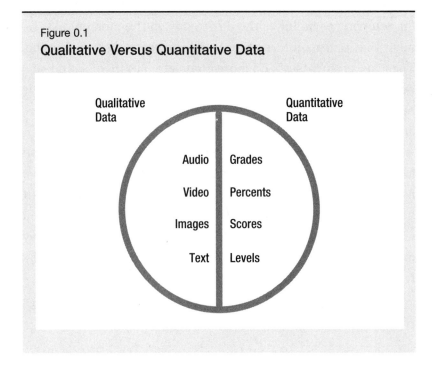

Figure 0.1
Qualitative Versus Quantitative Data

Qualitative
Data

Quantitative
Data

Audio | Grades

Video | Percents

Images | Scores

Text | Levels

With that in mind, digital portfolio assessment is an effective way to structure and analyze qualitative student learning results. This approach can help teachers embrace the messiness of teaching and learning in a way that better honors our craft. Digital portfolio assessment, when implemented successfully, can reveal a more complete description of our students as learners. In the process, parents and other teachers become partners in our students' learning journeys.

The organization of this book is intended to guide teachers toward building a comprehensive approach to using digital portfolios with students. We take it one step at a time. Chapter 1 offers a definition plus a vignette of digital portfolio assessment in action. This description creates a context for unpacking the three types of portfolios—performance (best work), progress (growth over time), and process (student reflections and experiences)—and how they are difficult to categorize. A brief history of portfolio assessments is also examined. Through this understanding, we develop the foundation for assessment literacy that we explore in the following chapters.

In Chapter 2, I make the case for implementing digital student portfolios in schools. The rationale focuses on both academic reasons and social and emotional benefits of this more authentic approach to assessment. I also share a few words of caution. With any significant pedagogical or practical change, there is a certain level of departure from prior practice. However, I believe that any challenges associated with adopting a portfolio assessment—with the help of technology—is worth the effort, especially considering the benefits.

In Chapter 3, we get started with using digital portfolios with students. Guidance is provided for how to assess the needs of your students, develop a yearlong plan for instruction, and select the digital tools to capture their best work within performance portfolios. This is a logical first step to implementing digital portfolios in the classroom. The success experienced at this stage can pave the way for integrating technology more powerfully in the future.

In Chapter 4, we delve deeper in portfolio assessments. Specifically, we look at how backward design, or planning with the end in mind, can be enhanced with progress, process, and performance portfolios. Instruction should be intentional to ensure that students arrive at essential understandings. This chapter offers suggestions for aligning portfolio assessment, both summative and formative, with standards. We will explore multiple examples of how a comprehensive portfolio assessment system can help teachers create more authentic pathways toward high-quality student learning outcomes.

In Chapter 5, I describe the larger process of going school-wide with digital portfolios. In my first book on digital student portfolios (Renwick, 2014), I shared the three-year journey my previous school took to integrating technology in our building. The lessons I learned from that experience, both positive and constructive, inform the steps I offer here for principals and teacher leaders. The overarching goal in this chapter is to ensure equity and agency for all students through the development of curriculum, along with consistent beliefs and practices.

In Chapter 6, we look beyond the construct of digital portfolio assessment. Specifically, I ask big questions, such as "How can students truly own their learning?" and "Could digital student portfolios replace more traditional forms of assessment?" The objective of this chapter is to challenge our thinking and consider students' learning lives beyond their K–12 experiences.

It is said that what gets measured is what gets done. I would add to this statement another adage: what we measure is what we value. For far too long, grades, scores, levels, and standardized tests have driven the conversation in education. Assumptions are made about students that are based on unreliable information and faulty logic. If we truly value the whole child—healthy, safe, engaged, supported, and challenged—then our assessments need to reflect this philosophy. Digital portfolios should not be seen as a panacea for all that ails assessment in schools today. However, what it can do is serve as the next step in doing better by our students, our families and communities, and society at large.

With that, let the journey begin!

Linked Activity: Build Professional Knowledge

When I wrote my first book on the topic of digital portfolios, it was partly because a resource on that topic didn't exist. I had to collect and curate many resources on the topics of portfolio assessment, 21st century learning, and teaching the whole child. This process was as important to increasing my knowledge as the actual act of writing the book.

Consider taking a similar learning journey. This resource does not contain all there is to know about digital portfolios. Use advanced Google search strategies with key phrases to discover new ideas on this subject. Collect and curate this information using online tools, such as Pinterest, Evernote, and LiveBinders. Share your findings with others, and come back to this information when you run into challenges while implementing digital portfolios. Building a dynamic body of knowledge is an important first step in becoming a lifelong learner in the 21st century.

Defining Digital Portfolios

"I did then what I knew how to do. Now that I know better, I do better."

—Maya Angelou

Too much assessment in schools today is done *to* students instead of *with* students. Even when the assessment reveals more than a score, the student or teacher does not have much say in the process. That said, within the context of the classroom, teachers still have considerable authority over how they can guide their students to improve daily. For example, through thoughtful language choices that are focused on a growth mindset, students can develop agency—the belief that things such as our intelligence and life's outcomes are changeable (Johnston, 2012). These teacher-student conversations bring students to focus on *what* they are doing instead of just *how* they are doing. In such a context, numbers and grades no longer direct these discussions.

In this chapter, we explore how digital portfolios can help students and teachers make this shift toward a partnership approach to assessment. A working definition, along with types and examples of digital portfolios, is offered to build a common understanding. We also look at the history of portfolio assessment in education, including why it seemed to disappear—along with reasons for its resurgence. The chapter ends with a framework for thinking about digital portfolio assessment through the lens of good pedagogy. Though technology is here to stay and has brought a lot of good into our world, the tenets of strong instruction are timeless.

Defining Digital Portfolios

Using technology to aid teaching and learning is not a new concept. Interactive whiteboards, the Internet, and wireless access are commonplace in schools. Recent technology, such as learning management systems like Edmodo and Schoology, has provided teachers with the ability to facilitate some classroom activities online. What is new is how technology can and should be leveraged to transform teaching and learning—instead of just enhancing it. This requires a shift in practice. Both teachers and students can improve in their work with the inclusion of digital tools when they are thoughtfully integrated with instruction.

Digital portfolio assessment is one such approach that could build a learning partnership. David Niguidula (2010) coined the term *digital student portfolios,* defined as "a multimedia collection of student work that provides evidence of a student's skills and knowledge" (p. 154). I've expanded on this definition and consider digital student portfolios to be dynamic, digital collections of information from many sources, in many forms, and with many purposes that better represent a student's understanding and learning experiences.

How we define digital student portfolios, though, is secondary to how we use the related technology in the classroom. Strong instruction with technology embedded as a necessary resource is preferable. For example, implementing a 1:1 program (i.e., one digital device per student) without any type of forethought, research, or planning does not lead to significant learning outcomes. In fact, such an approach could exacerbate achievement gaps for at-risk students who are not familiar with the technology (Toyoma, 2015). The change we want to see in schools—and that we hope technology will help facilitate—requires more than just a financial investment.

Three Types of Portfolios

Let's take a deeper look at the purposes of portfolios and the different types of portfolios that have been used in schools (Figure 1.1). Literacy professors Richard Allington and Patricia Cunningham (2006) offer clear definitions for this assessment tool and process (p. 179):

- Performance portfolios are collections of a student's best work, with the student taking the lead in the selection of the work and providing an explanation as to why they should be included.
- Process portfolios contain several versions of a selected work. Such a portfolio might hold early drafts of a paper or poem to show how the piece developed over time.
- Progress portfolios are often managed by teachers. They hold collections of work intended to illustrate children's development over time.

Bear in mind that regarding the different types of student portfolios, "few pure examples of any of these types exist" (Allington & Cunningham, 2006, p. 179). The vignette that follows is a good example. A teacher and a student celebrate a piece of

Figure 1.1
Different Types of Portfolios

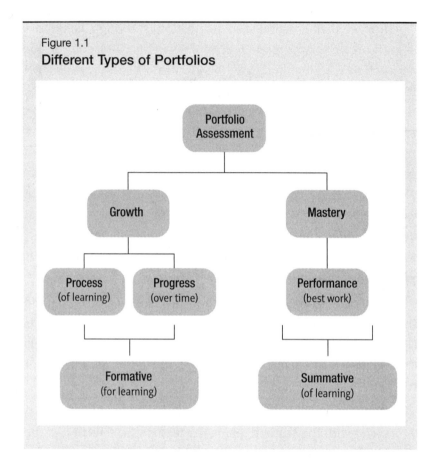

published writing (a performance), yet it also serves as a point of instruction (progress). This combination of a showcase portfolio that is student driven and a benchmark portfolio that is teacher directed can be referred to as a "collaborative portfolio" (Jenkins, 1996).

In my experience, I have found it helpful when getting started with digital portfolios to categorize them based on purpose. We can refer to the three types of portfolios in terms of "best work" or "growth." Students, families, and colleagues typically understand this terminology better. Best-work portfolios are student driven and include collections of students' best work. Growth portfolios are teacher directed and represent students' development over time. Regardless of the type of portfolio, opportunities for documenting and sharing student learning can happen at any time. Teachers need to take advantage of these situations and worry about how to categorize them later, if at all.

To provide some context for digital portfolios, the following passage describes a small moment in which a teacher (Janice) is conferencing with a student (Calleigh). Janice video-recorded her writing conference using an application called FreshGrade (www. freshgrade.com). This conference was eventually shared with Calleigh's family through the application. Each piece selected by Calleigh throughout the school year is also saved within FreshGrade to show growth over time. Previously, Janice had provided instruction through minilessons on writing strategies. She was already aware of her students' writing abilities through a fall schoolwide writing assessment. The results of that assessment were quantitative (i.e., numerical) and based on one rubric. However, Janice's success in the writing conference was measured through Calleigh's ability to monitor her own growth in writing and take more responsibility for the results.

In the Classroom with Janice and Calleigh

Calleigh, a 2nd grader, sits down with her teacher, Janice Heyroth, to prepare for an assessment. This is a regularly scheduled conference during the middle of the school year; Janice meets with each student six times a year to reflect on a piece of writing in their digital portfolios. At the beginning of the year, students completed a reading and writing survey, which was uploaded and shared with students' families via FreshGrade. The information gleaned from that survey gave Janice information about each student's dispositions toward reading and writing. Questions such as "What types of books does your child enjoy reading on this/her own?" and "Does your child enjoy writing? Why or why not?" gave insights into how students approached literacy in their lives. It also informed her future instruction, such as generating writing ideas and topics students could choose to explore if they needed more support.

Elbows on the table, Calleigh props her head on her hands as her teacher spreads out some of her own writing. Because it is the middle of the school year, Calleigh's folder already contains multiple compositions. Janice encourages Calleigh to locate a recently published piece she is proud of. She selects one, and then Janice starts off their assessment with a question: "So, what are some things you are doing well?"

Calleigh doesn't hesitate. She states, "Handwriting." Calleigh pulls an older piece of writing from her folder and compares it with a more recent entry to show the difference. Janice listens and smiles while she writes down Calleigh's response in her conferring notebook.

Janice prompts, "What else?" and then silently waits and allows Calleigh the time she needs to look back at her writing and find other points to highlight. After a few seconds, she responds, "I don't know."

Janice acknowledges Calleigh's honesty and follows up with more specific language. She says, "Well, I have noticed a lot of areas where I think you're doing well in your writing. First, you stayed organized with your writing. Did you notice that?"

Calleigh tentatively nods.

Janice then says, "Do you know what I mean by staying organized in your writing?"

Calleigh hesitates and then smiles as she responds, "No."

"Okay . . . did you stay on topic?"

"Yeah"

"What is your topic about?"

"Going to Florida."

"Right. It's all about going to Florida. Did you tell me about what you did first and go all the way through to the end?"

"Yes."

The conversation continues, and while this assessment is taking place, the rest of the students in the classroom are busy independently reading and writing, working on self-guided vocabulary activities, or using computers to listen to narrated digital stories. At one point in the assessment, Janice starts to make a suggestion ("Would it have made sense . . ."), stops herself, and then restarts her inquiry: "Why did you start your real narrative in this way?" Calleigh shares that she started her story by describing an important scene during her visit to Florida. This is a strategy for developing a lead that she learned during whole-group writing instruction. Janice makes sure to note this connection between teaching and learning in her notebook.

The assessment closes with Janice asking Calleigh what she would like to continue working on with her writing. This time, she waits 15 seconds for a response.

Finally, Calleigh says, "Spaces."

Janice pauses and then responds, "Actually, your spacing is fine. The same with your spelling and handwriting—everything looks great. Let's take a look at your ending, though. 'Our trip to Florida was fun and exciting.' How could you have spiced things up and made your ending more memorable?"

Calleigh struggles with how to respond. Janice reminds her that endings can often resemble leads. With this information in hand, Janice makes a note to prepare future minilessons that address endings. Janice finishes up her time with Calleigh by showing her how to upload her writing to FreshGrade so her parents can see her work.

Assessment in Context

To understand how digital portfolio assessment can inform teaching and learning, let's unpack the conference scenario between Janice and Calleigh.

Relationships as a Foundation for Learning

Relationships are the cornerstone of all teaching and learning. Consider the initial interaction between Janice and her students. When Calleigh stated "I don't know" to Janice, she was being honest. She was willing to reveal her lack of knowledge about what good writing might resemble. Janice responded professionally, instead of "What do you mean you don't know? We covered this yesterday." She saw this admission as an opportunity for celebration and for instruction. Janice pointed out Calleigh's strengths in organization and how her conventions and presentation made her writing more readable. This opened the door for feedback and growth, especially when they started talking about her ending.

It is hard to learn from someone whom we do not respect or particularly care for. Learners must have trust in their teachers. Making mistakes puts us in a vulnerable position, and when we're forced to admit that we don't know something, we open ourselves up to potential criticism. This can be good situation if a high level of trust and a positive relationship have been developed between student and teacher. Students need to see their teachers as credible and reliable to be able to accept feedback about their performance.

Janice understood this. She maintained her relationship with Calleigh as a way to help her student grow as a writer. This trust was developed through genuine celebration and thoughtful interaction. In addition, it allowed Janice to document this assessment through a digital portfolio tool.

Assessment and Agency

As the writing conference transitioned from celebration to observation and feedback, Janice caught herself about to make a suggestion. This would not have been the end of the world, but it also would not have given Calleigh enough credit for her potential. By rephrasing her suggestion into a question, Janice allowed for Calleigh to take more ownership of her writing. Asking a question that begins, "Would it have made sense . . ." is leading and teacher directed. Unfortunately, this is much too typical in classrooms today. The alternative approach ("Why did you start your narrative . . .") casts the student in the position of expert and requires them to justify their decisions. Calleigh was asked to support her own writing decisions, which were the result of strategies previously taught in the classroom. Calleigh was the lead assessor in this situation, and Janice was acting as a coach looking to build independence with her student. Bringing an authentic audience into this conference heightened the importance of Calleigh's work.

Clear Criteria for Success

Near the end of the writing conference, it became clear to Janice that Calleigh lacked the knowledge to develop informed writing goals for the next time they met. At that point, she recognized the need to be more prescriptive in her feedback. Her suggestion was brief and built on prior knowledge (using leads to build endings), yet she didn't spend a lot of time on it. Using this gap in knowledge as information to drive her instruction, Janice began to plan a future minilesson (or two) on endings. Chances are high that if Calleigh, who happened to be one of the stronger 2nd grade writers, needed more instruction in this area, then so did her classmates.

It's hard for students to meet expectations in any discipline if the criteria for success are unclear. Assessment is effective when teachers can provide instruction during the process of learning. The function of the conference was for Calleigh to identify her best writing within the context of current work and the standards of excellence conveyed by Janice. Their conversation was about celebrating success and moving forward as a writer. Calleigh was therefore positioned to consider improvement instead of simply being evaluated. With this in mind, assessments should focus on teachers and students working together with a clear set of criteria to get better. How better to capture this work than through technology?

Students of Our Own Instruction

The video recording of their conference for Calleigh's digital portfolio served as an artifact of reflection, self-assessment, and goal setting. Both the video reflection and image of her writing were combined within FreshGrade and shared with her parents. They were able to watch the conference and read Calleigh's writing on their smartphone, tablet, or computer. In addition, they could leave a simple, supportive comment on the digital artifact, or even go deeper and emulate Janice's language by offering specific feedback and asking thoughtful questions.

Just as important, Janice later watched the footage and evaluated her own practice within FreshGrade. While Calleigh's parents could appreciate her growth by comparing her submitted work online, Janice could critique her own interactions with her student and assess whether her feedback moved Calleigh forward as a learner. Janice saw this footage as essential data to inform her instruction—information just as valuable as any rubric or test might offer. In using digital portfolios in this way, the teacher becomes the learner as much as the student.

Additional Examples of Digital Portfolios

The following vignettes offer more examples of digital portfolios in the context of the classroom. Consider these three scenarios and how they might apply to your grade level and/or discipline.

Scenario #1: Barry, a high school English teacher, finds his students' writing lacking in both skill and voice. He therefore makes the decision to use Google Drive for his students' writing projects throughout the school year. The classroom has access to one cart of Chromebooks. Because of the one-device-per-student ratio in his classroom, every learner has access to his or her digital writing and projects within this web-based software and storage system. Students are taught how to create folders within Google Drive for different writing projects (created with both Google Docs and Slides). At specific times during the school year, students are expected to select a piece of writing that represents their best work and post it to their performance portfolio, hosted on a Google Site. Every student is expected not only to select and publish a piece of writing but also to offer feedback for classmates. In addition, Barry has connected with another classroom in a different state to expand the number of opportunities for his students to communicate with a meaningful audience. The clarity provided by the teacher on how to use Google Drive to organize the process of writing, along with an authentic audience that could facilitate feedback in an online environment, offered relevance and motivation for students to increase their voice and better apply their skills.

Scenario #2: Lori, a middle school math teacher, is not seeing her students transfer their learning to new situations. They are respectful and attentive during class, but when presented with a similar yet novel problem, the students struggle to apply their knowledge and skills.

Lori believes that the missing link between instruction and understanding is the lack of integration of the recommended eight mathematics practices in her curriculum (Common Core State Standards):

1. Make sense of problems and persevere in solving them.
2. Reason abstractly and quantitatively.
3. Construct viable arguments and critique the reasoning of others.
4. Model with mathematics.
5. Use appropriate tools strategically.
6. Attend to precision.
7. Look for and make use of structure.
8. Look for and express regularity in repeated reasoning.

For students to become more self-aware of how these practices help them in mathematics, Lori decides to have her classes reflect daily about their learning. She signs up for a Kidblog (www. kidblog.org) account. Students have their own blogs to write about how they used one or more of the mathematical practices during the lesson. Lori teaches her students how to categorize and tag their posts based on the topic of study and mathematic practices. This math journaling happens at the end of the lesson and serves multiple purposes: to give students the opportunity to reflect on their math work through writing, to reveal their understanding of the day's lesson for Lori to read, and to provide a window for parents who want to better understand how their children are doing in school. As homework, instead of a worksheet, students are often expected to respond to at least two classmates' posts in the comments. This type of work seems more authentic, and it promotes the idea of a community of learners rather than kids competing with one another in learning.

Scenario #3: Cathy, an elementary school teacher, finds her reading conference notebook cumbersome. She wants to be smarter about documenting students' reading goals and taking notes as she talks one on one with students during independent reading time. Cathy learns about CCPensieve, an online conferring notebook application that is connected to the Daily 5 literacy workshop model (Boushey & Moser, 2014). Within this web-based software, teachers can quickly move from student to student and find personalized assessment data that show their growth as readers. Using CCPensieve as a progress portfolio, there's no need to leaf though a thick binder full of papers to find reading goals, lists of books read, or strategy notes for the next student conference. Cathy can quickly see a snapshot of all of her students on the main page of her digital account. In addition, because the information is stored online, she can access this information from any computer or mobile device with an Internet connection.

Another advantage is how CCPensieve allows others to be involved in the process. Students can use the information about their reading lives to gain a better understanding of their accomplishments and next steps. Parents are able to ascertain their child's learning progress because of how the qualitative data is organized and shared out via email. Other teachers can be invited to view and add to a student's progress portfolio. CCPensieve becomes an additional way for colleagues to communicate and collaborate without actually being in the same room. Cathy, her colleagues, and students' family members are all partners in students' journeys toward becoming lifelong readers.

These three examples have much in common. First, each scenario identifies the specific **access** necessary for teachers and students to be successful. For example, when a 1:1 student-to-technology ratio is required, only then is it provided. Second, the **purpose** for the inclusion of technology is prompted by pedagogy. Whether it is the need to facilitate peer feedback, to include students in the process of goal setting and reflection, or to better communicate students' learning progress, the rationale for the inclusion of digital tools is steeped in learning. Third, students' learning becomes visible outside the classroom. In all three examples, families and peers are brought in to the learning process. Because of this **audience**, the work automatically becomes more authentic and meaningful. These common elements serve to frame technology integration for educators, shared later in this chapter.

Understanding Portfolio Assessment

The previous example of digital portfolios in action (Janice and Calleigh) is a powerful portrait of what's possible with digital portfolio assessment in the classroom. To understand this process, it is helpful to understand the concept of assessment as well as the origins of portfolios in education.

Assessment 101

Assessment is the form, not the function. Teachers assess student learning to discover if their understanding of a concept or ability to demonstrate a skill is at a proficient level, and if not, then to respond accordingly. To understand how portfolio assessment has evolved to the present day, it is helpful to understand assessment in general and how portfolios have attempted to capture the qualitative information in the classroom that can better represent the whole child.

Assessment can be defined as the process and tools used to reveal information about a learner's progress and achievement. As teachers, we assign certain values to levels of development that a student most likely has attained as a reader, writer, and thinker. The more information we can glean regarding a student's ability, the better and broader a picture we have to make instructional and curricular decisions.

Of course, too much information might result in data overload. A certain limit must be determined so we remain focused on teaching and learning rather than on gathering and organizing. A good analogy is a visit to the doctor's office. Your doctor will take your blood pressure, listen to your heart, check your ears and eyes, and so on. However, he or she is not going to take a blood sample if the initial assessments don't warrant it. There are many correlations between the two situations. Age, expected cognitive development, experience, and other outside factors (e.g., background knowledge, parental support) also come into play as we build an understanding of our students' strengths, needs, and interests.

The concept of assessment is often divided into two types: formative and summative. The simplest comparison between formative and summative assessment is that formative is assessment *for* learning and summative is assessment *of* learning (Black & Wiliam, 1998). If you break down these words etymologically, *inform* is related to *formative*. This information would therefore inform our instruction. An example might be exit cards/tickets, where students respond to a question to check for understanding at the end of the lesson. Their work isn't graded. Exit cards/ tickets are used to simply inform the teacher's instruction for the future.

By contrast, *summary* is closely related to *summative,* which would imply that data from this type of assessment are collected after the learning has occurred. Your typical unit tests and performance tasks would fall into this category. Figure 1.2 expands on this comparison.

Figure 1.2
Formative Versus Summative Assessment

Qualities of Formative Assessment	Qualities of Summative Assessment
along the way, everyday instructional practice	at the end, after learning has occurred, with no chance to redo
daily practice toward a product	product only
immediate feedback for the teacher and learner	feedback for both the teacher and learner often delayed
informs the teacher and the learner so instruction and practice can be adjusted the next day	informs future instruction and course design
focuses on the task; geared toward understanding	focuses on the individual's mastery of information at specific point in time
allows assessor to get and give immediate feedback to improve student achievement	frequently used as a way to sift and sort students for placement; serves as a gatekeeper for advanced classes and electives

Source: From *So What Do They Really Know? Assessment That Informs Teaching and Learning,* by C. Tovani, 2010, Portsmouth, NH: Stenhouse. Copyright 2010 by Stenhouse. Reprinted with permission.

Cris Tovani accompanies this comparison with a helpful analogy (2010). When she speaks with teachers, she often compares formative and summative assessments with athletics. Practice time is an opportunity for coaches to provide explicit feedback based on current performance. At game time, however, very little feedback is given except for the final score. Much more time is devoted to practice, where the goal is to improve. The summative assessments (game time) are more infrequent opportunities to "show me what you know."

These two types of assessments clearly work in concert within the arena of athletics. Yet this connection is often lacking in the classroom. If formative assessments are there to guide instruction for learning, then both student and teacher need to know the learning target(s) they must hit (Moss & Brookhart, 2012). To know the target, a clear understanding of the standard of excellence needs to be developed and conveyed. If the district and state (summative) assessments are aligned with these standards, then the target should hopefully be clear. And with that destination in mind, formative assessments can provide a pathway for learners to achieve strong growth and eventually mastery.

A Brief History of Portfolio Assessment

Portfolios have long been used to document student learning. Portfolios came into prominence during the 1980s and 90s as an authentic assessment tool for writing workshop. This approach was spearheaded by educators such as Donald Graves and Sheila Valencia (Jenkins, 1996). These innovators in literacy instruction believed that reading and writing were too complex to be evaluated through letter grades or single scores. With that in mind, an authentic approach to portfolio assessment sought to "minimize the distance between instruction and assessment" (Valencia & Place, 1994, p. 154). Portfolios in the context of literacy can be a better approach to assessment, as reading and writing rely on qualitative results to gauge growth and achievement.

Around the same time, education was also exploring the use of portfolio assessment for groups of students with specific needs. For example, Moya and O'Malley (1994) reported on some of the benefits of using portfolios for English language learners, including a greater ability to focus on the process of learning (instead of only on outcomes) and the ability to tailor assessment to the needs of each student. In addition, with the emergence of new learning theories, such as multiple intelligences, educators and researchers saw a new pathway for leveraging portfolio assessment to capture, reflect upon, and share student learning artifacts. Educational researchers such as Evangeline Stefanakis (2002) advocated for the use of portfolio assessment to document students' intelligence beyond the core disciplines. Students who demonstrated strength in physical education and music, for instance, were offered new opportunities to convey their understandings through a more authentic approach to assessment. As an example, students could use a video recording from a choir concert to show proficiency in their musical abilities. An assessment such as this, facilitated through technology, is better aligned with the expectations for the discipline.

Given these benefits, it still is not surprising that portfolio assessment has fallen out of favor in schools. This more authentic approach to assessment also demands more time and attention; reflection, self-assessment, and goal setting are critical components of the process. With large class sizes, less support, and more resources devoted to standardized assessments, limitations are placed on educators who might want to facilitate portfolio assessment. As veteran literacy educator and author Regie Routman notes, "I remember decades ago when portfolio assessment was all the rage. Then it died a slow death because it was overwhelming for teachers to implement with their students, not to mention all the time it took" (personal communication). Another challenge is the qualitative nature of this approach. For example, student writing is more difficult to assign a grade or score to than, say, a solution to a math problem. The draw of an easier-to-implement assessment system that relied mainly on numbers and symbols gave way instead.

With recent advances in technology, portfolio assessment has experienced a resurgence in popularity. Many technology companies now offer digital portfolio tools to use in the classroom. The biggest reason is the capacity of technology to capture, house, and share artifacts of student learning online. The advent of the Internet, along with a bevy of affordable mobile devices, has caused educators to rethink student work as more than only a physical object or file. In using digital tools to capture student thinking and progress, students' learning journeys start to become alive. We can hear the confidence in their voice when giving a speech and see their enthusiasm when presenting on a research topic in school. In addition, technology has allowed students to become better involved in the assessment process itself. Tablets and laptops put in the hands of learners give them more opportunities to document, reflect upon, and publish their work. This access to share and assess growth and best work is more easily captured with digital portfolios. Finally, these tools inform families about their children's current understandings and future goals. How digital portfolios are integrated into the classroom is an important next step.

A Framework for Digital Portfolios

Digital portfolios, these dynamic repositories of student learning artifacts, stand in contrast with the symbols that have typically represented learning in schools, including grades and test scores. Quantitative assessment results are static and unresponsive. They draw little attention to the overall learning process. Numbers and symbols are not without some worth. Grades on high school transcripts still act as prerequisites for acceptance to higher education. Test scores provide a snapshot of a school's general achievement levels. However, these assessments are instruments that can, at best, make rough estimates about a student's or school's achievement levels. Still, numbers and symbols are much easier to collect, organize, and analyze.

Qualitative assessment results need processes and protocols so teachers and students can more systematically implement them in classrooms. In my previous work (Renwick, 2014, 2015), I offered a basic framework for assessing the effect that technology can have on student learning: access, purpose, and audience. *Access* is the availability for students to use connected tools, discover new knowledge, and tap into currently unavailable resources. Access can also take into account how technology modifies and accommodates content and tasks for students with specific needs. *Purpose* is defined as the reason for utilizing technology in the context of learning. It also should offer a rationale for the work in which students engage while at school and in their lives. *Audience* includes anyone who can view and celebrate students' learning, as well as provide feedback to promote thinking. The three tenets of necessary use of technology are described in Figure 1.3.

Access, purpose, audience: within these three tenets of a digital integration framework, we are more likely to experience success in the classroom. Technology comes and goes. With a strong understanding of portfolio assessment in general, we can better align the digital tools to meet our students' true needs. Technology should support the learning, not the other way around.

Linked Activity: Using a Framework to Reflect on Current Practice

Think about your current learning environment for students, including the discipline(s) you teach, assessment practices used in your classroom, resources available, and schoolwide expectations.

Figure 1.3

Access, Purpose, and Audience

Access	It is **nice** to purchase one type of device for every learner, provide initial training, and allow staff and students to explore what's possible.	It is **necessary** to assess infrastructure, school needs, and student needs as well as purchase specific tools and schedule ongoing training.
Purpose	It is **nice** to use trial-and-error with the technology and select a curriculum unit or lesson that allows for its use.	It is **necessary** to design curriculum focused on essential knowledge and skills and apply technology within the learning progression.
Audience	It is **nice** to house student work on the devices or in the cloud for easy retrieval.	It is **necessary** to publish student work for those outside the classroom to view and give feedback and affirmation.

Considering your context, respond to the following questions to help you reflect on your current practice and what's possible for the future.

1. What type of **access** do your students have to technology in your classroom? Specifically, what is the wireless situation? How many and what types of devices are available? What is your district's current policy on sharing student information in an online space? What needs should be addressed?

2. Given your current teaching assignment, what entry point in your curriculum makes the most sense for integrating

digital portfolios? That is, what would be the **purpose** of incorporating technology within your discipline? How will student learning benefit from this inclusion?

3. If access is strong and a purpose has been identified, who will be the **audience** that will be celebrating and assessing students' work? Will family members be the main recipients for looking at and commenting on their learning? How might peers be involved in recognizing and offering feedback for what's posted and shared?

Learner Profile: John Spencer

John Spencer is a professor of educational technology within the School of Education at George Fox University in Portland, Oregon. Prior to that, he was a middle school social studies and digital journalism teacher in the Phoenix, Arizona area. His school had many Spanish speakers in a state that demanded all school work be read and completed in English. John is also the author of *Launch: Using Design Thinking to Boost Creativity and Bring Out the Maker in Every Student* (2016).

Questions in each chapter's Learner Profile are adapted from *The Action Research Guidebook: A Four-Stage Process for Educators and School Teams* (Sagor, 2010, pp. 37–38).

Why did you introduce digital portfolio assessment in your classroom?

I started digital portfolios early on in my career. The purpose was to have a classroom assessment system that mirrored what professionals and artists (creative types) do in the real world. They do not take tests—they select their best work to showcase and explain why. Not aware of other resources available, my colleagues and I started with portfolios from scratch.

Our first step was teaching students how to choose their learning artifacts during the school year and reflect upon them. This led to having the students start to document their growth over time, which then led to students self-selecting goals to work toward for the future. This is ideal summative work in the creative fields, where people make plans for the future based on what they have accomplished so far and where they want to grow.

In what way(s) were the effects of implementing digital portfolios in school unique or unusual?

There were positive effects about using a portfolio process with students. By celebrating their work once a quarter (when they put entries in their portfolios), they started to see themselves as learners—as creative people who can accomplish projects. There were changes in their self-concept, not necessarily in their confidence, but in becoming more reflective individuals.

There was also an increase in metacognition because of the time given for students to reflect on their learning. When the growth piece was added, a lot of the power in portfolios came in having the students articulate what they learned and how. It was on their terms and facilitated by the teacher. This portfolio process led into goal setting, which was a phenomenal thing. Had I stayed in my position as a social studies teacher (instead of transitioning to an encore class), I would have scheduled this goal setting to happen weekly where it became a habit for the school.

How would you describe the characteristics of the products from the digital portfolio work and of the educators who were involved?

Working on a teaching team at the middle level, we could really see the students as learners. We got a great snapshot of each person; seeing their strengths and areas for growth were documented in multiple disciplines. When I started teaching digital journalism toward the end of my K–12 teaching career, the ability to collaborate with colleagues became more challenging. Career-based courses such as journalism lend themselves to a portfolio style of assessment. What they created, such as news reports and reviews, was already online and selected because of its quality. Writing in multiple genres happens naturally. The work is relevant. When schools and teachers select units of study focused on a genre, such as persuasive and expository writing, the learning can become more about completing the assignments than about creating an actual product for an authentic audience.

While we didn't receive any training on how to implement portfolios when our school went to standards-based grading, portfolios made a whole lot more sense. We were no longer assigning a number or a letter to student work. Instead, we looked at specific knowledge and skills in which students had to show proficiency and then built assessments and developed the curriculum around them. Both standard-based grading and portfolio assessment do a better job of showing a student's learning journey over time.

Q&A What resources were used to support the use of digital portfolios?

Going digital with student portfolios demanded technological resources. The biggest benefits were improved communication with families and bringing in a more authentic audience. Our team used Weebly (www.weebly.com) for students to showcase their learning online. My wife went to school with one of the developers of Weebly. When she shared this new tool with me, I thought, "Hey, our kids could use this for their digital portfolios." We had been using Dreamweaver, which required students to actually build the website in addition to posting their work. Through Weebly, our students could focus on the learning. One of the outcomes of using online portfolios is the positive digital footprint they create though the process. If the portfolios do not stay with them after graduating, they aren't as real.

Q&A What specific outcomes do you attribute to the use of digital portfolios?

The positive outcomes of a portfolio assessment culture are not reserved just for students. Professionalism was also increased when we, as teachers, collaborated on this initiative. I would not have worked as closely with my colleagues on my team if portfolio assessment were not a part of our work.

Q&A In your opinion, what other factors contributed to the achievement of these outcomes?

The support from our administrators, such as providing time to discuss student learning and develop authentic assessments, was necessary to allow this to happen. This is in addition to the district's decision to use a more student-friendly reporting system (i.e., standards-based grading). Another factor that led to students becoming more mindful and reflective about their learning included a school culture in which teacher leadership was honored and encouraged.

Q&A What problems did you encounter when developing or introducing digital portfolios?

Portfolio assessment does not come without its issues. Any significant change in how school looks and works for students will have bumps in the road. For us, most of the problems stemmed from the technology itself. Having students upload their multimedia creations, such as videos and images, proved to be challenging for all of us. Bandwidth strength and different types of files affected this process. Also, we as teachers had to make sure we were compliant with FERPA (Family Educational Rights and Privacy Act) and COPPA (Children's Online Privacy Protection Act) guidelines regarding student privacy and information. Providing universal access to all students regarding technology can also prove to be a roadblock. This access includes language barriers, as a number of our students and their families spoke Spanish as their primary language. Ensuring that student learning was communicated was not an easy process.

 What else do you think a teacher or school should know before implementing digital portfolios?

First, choose the digital portfolio platform wisely. It makes a big difference as to how easy it is for students to upload their work, reflect on it, and set goals for the future. Second, show students how to curate digital portfolios. Don't assume they know how because they are familiar with digital tools. Make exemplars or find strong examples of what student portfolios can and should look like. Teach portfolio assessment like you would teach any other complex task. Third, do your homework on student privacy laws. Find out what the district policy states about digital portfolio assessment, and make sure you have administrative support. Finally, if possible, facilitate portfolio assessment with a team of teachers—or the entire school. Hold one another accountable to do this type of work, which does not come naturally for those who are used to a more traditional approach to education. You learn a lot more about your students when everyone is contributing to their learning journey—the student included!

2

Making a Case
for Digital Portfolios

"Relationships are the agents of change."

—Dr. Bruce Perry

As a school principal, I helped facilitate an action research course for district teachers. One teacher wanted to explore blogging as a writing tool in her classroom. The professor who taught the course asked her, "So why do want your students to blog?" She paused, not sure how to answer the question. Blogging is an excellent tool for writing and bringing in an authentic audience. However, without an ability to convey the necessity of this integration, an innovation such as this tends to fall flat. Without purpose, change is fleeting.

In the first chapter, we defined portfolio assessment, explored what a digital portfolio could look like in the classroom, and examined digital portfolios within a technology integration framework. In this chapter, I make the case that implementing digital student portfolios is a necessary action and should become a part of a teacher's assessment process. Each of the following reasons is accompanied with explanations and/or examples in this chapter:

1. Celebrate all students as learners.
2. Improve home-school communication.
3. Facilitate better feedback.
4. Highlight the process of learning.
5. Demonstrate progress over time.
6. Guide students to become self-directed learners.
7. Maximize formative assessment.
8. Integrate speaking and listening.
9. Advocate for every student.
10. Work smarter as a teacher.

To know what we are getting into, responses to common concerns and challenges regarding implementation of digital portfolios are also provided. By understanding the purpose, we gain the motivation to ensure technology integration initiatives such as digital portfolios are successful for students.

Reason #1: Celebrate All Students as Learners

To expect the best from our students, we have to start with success. Acknowledging all the potential they have to offer paves the way for future growth. Think about your favorite teachers and what made them memorable. Didn't you work the hardest for them because they recognized all that you had to offer? This isn't about dolloping spoonfuls of unsubstantiated praise on students. Rather, it is looking at students through the lens of what's possible for them as learners—instead of immediately identifying their deficits.

I remember when my children were toddlers and learning to understand the world around them. When they started to talk, my wife and I never called them out for their mistakes. Instead, we recognized their efforts while scaffolding their responses with what they were trying to say and convey (e.g., "Did you say *dee*? Yes, the *dog* is barking at the squirrel outside. You said it!"). This language comes natural to most young parents. So what happens when children get older?

In a word: school. All of a sudden, kids are compared to one another. Instead of collaboration, competition typically takes over. Whether it is the visible groupings of students based on reading levels, the clip charts that admonish our most active learners, or the school data walls that tell teachers what they already know about their students, these unhealthy comparisons can lead to a decrease in students' sense of self-worth and a lack of engagement with learning in general.

What digital portfolio assessment provides for students is a more level playing field. No longer are we pigeonholing kids into one, narrow way of showing their learning. Instead, they can speak their understanding and record it with various digital tools. They can video record a demonstration of their new knowledge or skills and post it online for others to see. They can write about their experiences in a preferred way that helps them express themselves comfortably and clearly. Whatever approach they take, the limits have been lifted regarding performance assessment and what it means to be successful.

Reason #2: Improve Home-School Communication

I believe that what students bring home in their backpacks becomes their family's perception of what occurs at school. If your child's backpack were full of only math fact practice sheets, corrected reading quizzes, and graded content exams, what would be your interpretation? Parents might make the (hopefully) incorrect assumption that all their children do at school is comply with teachers' directions and dutifully take the predetermined, one-size-fits-all assessments to show what they know.

Because you are reading this book, my guess is that you are not comfortable with our families or community members having this point of view. Nevertheless, without an alternative way to communicate student learning, we create a perception vacuum. Digital portfolios offer a better system. Students' regular efforts at demonstrating their knowledge, understandings, and dispositions are all on display for families to witness as they develop. This formative process breathes life into an otherwise mundane method of reporting student learning.

By developing a digital portfolio with students, we create a better representation of who they are as learners. Portfolio assessment is a mosaic of their understandings, reflections, and attempts at meeting personal goals. Capturing these artifacts opens up our classroom doors to important audiences. In addition, students come to see themselves in a more accurate way—as complex learners who are unique and always striving to become better. The importance of the connection made between home and school—facilitated through digital portfolios—cannot be overstated.

Reason #3: Facilitate Better Feedback

Feedback is critical for learning. Without it, we have no idea if we are improving. Feedback can be defined as the flow of information between teacher and learner or between learners that informs current performance and next steps. It should be a "recipe for future instruction" (Wiliam, 2011, p. 121). Feedback can take a variety of forms. For example, our interactions with students during guided practice can offer a lot of information— from students' responses to our questions, to the conversations they have with their peers, to their facial expressions and body language. All of this can serve to inform teaching and learning— but how?

Digital student portfolios offer teachers and students a way to facilitate feedback more successfully. Consider the following example. Students are struggling with reading fluency (i.e., the ability to read text with expression, at a reasonable rate, and with understanding). The teacher, recognizing a lack of awareness among her students, decides to record her students once a week while they are reading. The videos are then shared with the students' families via digital notifications. They can hear their prosody (pace and rhythm) and enunciation (pronunciation) as they listen to themselves read aloud. Each week, this authentic artifact of their progress is a topic of conversation at home and school. After watching themselves on the recordings, students start to see and hear for themselves why fluency is critical for understanding.

The way that digital tools can capture true learning—in the moment—calls into question some of the more traditional literacy assessments currently used in schools. Which assessment helps students better understand their own abilities? If we agree that learners should be the lead assessors in the classroom, then what tools will best allow that to happen? Digital portfolios can change the game when it comes to students taking ownership of the data that is captured. Indeed, this information can be the motivation a student needs to improve.

Reason #4: Highlight the Process of Learning

A favorite biography of mine is Walter Isaacson's *Steve Jobs* (2011). What made the story of Jobs's life so compelling was not that he was a pioneer in the computer industry or that he revolutionized how people listen to music. What was most interesting was the road he traveled to get to that point. Jobs's biological parents abandoned him. He dropped out of college—though continued to attend courses that interested him, such as calligraphy.

Jobs eventually became a successful business leader, but he was fired by his own board of directors due to his caustic personality. These setbacks made the ultimate successes of his journey more rewarding.

What digital portfolios provide for learners is an opportunity to showcase their best work *and* highlight the journey they took to get there. Learning is no longer merely an abstract outcome of the process; it becomes visible. In addition, the audience is not limited to the teacher. Family members, peers, and the larger community can become "readers" of a student's narrative. There is also a focus on the importance of striving toward one's personal goals while becoming more aware of that growth. Students learn to think critically about what they produced and take action from that reflection.

A case in point: Teachers at my previous school had received training in specific instructional strategies for teaching the process of writing. Part of the expectation for that training was to include students' prewriting, plans, and drafts behind their final products when teachers posted their work in the classroom or hallway.

When our consultant came back for the second round of training in the late fall, she did an environmental walk of the school. Only the final products were visible. "Where are the plans?" she asked. The teachers looked nervously at one another, not sure what to say. She continued, "We need to communicate to the entire school community that writing does not come out of thin air." After that, we regularly shared the entire journey students took to create their final products.

Prioritizing the process of learning does not mean devaluing the final product students produce. It is about understanding that learning outcomes are largely a result of the time and thought spent developing the knowledge, skills, and dispositions on display in the end product. If teachers want to truly promote a "growth mindset" in their classrooms, then we need to shift our focus. When we take the time to visit with students, discuss the journey they took to achieve their goals, and celebrate their accomplishments along the way, we convey what we truly value as educators. Digital portfolios help with this shift.

Reason #5: Demonstrate Progress over Time

Too often, our lesson plans and units of study can serve as isolated activities in the eyes of our students. Connections between what happened yesterday and what is to come are lost. Instead of a progression of teaching and learning that align with larger goals and objectives, students begin to view instruction as happening in silos, separated by disciplines, periods, and quarters. This fragmentation of teaching can leave students wondering about the importance of what they are learning and how it connects with their lives and the world around them.

Digital portfolios can serve as an antidote to this type of educational compartmentalization. When teachers take the time to guide students' focus on their past work, their current abilities, and their future goals, their work becomes a seamless progression of learning. Consider the first example in this book. The teacher, Janice, started her writing conference by focusing on her student's strengths as a writer. This prompted her student, Calleigh, to think back about what she was already doing well, which connected her thinking to prior knowledge. Then Janice noticed and named skills and strategies that were being utilized. This was followed up by questions that helped Calleigh reflect on possible areas of growth. Finally, the conference concluded with goals to work on and document within a digital portfolio tool.

This vignette describes what can be facilitated within a classroom when the teacher values learning as a continuous journey over time. Assessment in these types of classrooms is not an event; it serves to guide students toward a meaningful end that will showcase their potential and achieve their personal goals. The journey is revealed when portfolios are utilized to capture those pathways toward success. Teachers have to give students the tools, time, and feedback to help them self-assess their progress and unpack the process.

Reason #6: Guide Students to Become Self-Directed Learners

Teacher-directed assessments can be useful for highlighting students' strengths and areas for growth. This leads to more responsive instruction and a better understanding of a child's abilities. By moving the role of assessor from teacher to student, schools can see even greater gains in learning. When students are put in charge of their own learning journey through reflective questioning and goal setting, they have more ownership in the process. They put themselves on the hook for achieving at higher levels and are therefore more likely to experience success.

I observed this process with my own daughter when she was in 1st grade. Using a built-in tablet camera, her teacher recorded their writing conference, which began with my daughter reading her own writing aloud. (The topic was her upcoming birthday party.) Next, they panned the camera over to the rubric used to guide the assessment.

Her teacher asked, "How do you feel you did on this writing?" My daughter pointed to the smiley face that served as a self-rating symbol on her reflection sheet.

"What about your writing are you really proud of?" The teacher motioned toward a bank of phrases from which my daughter could select (which also served as criteria for high-quality work at the 1st-grade level). After they identified a strength, her teacher asked her to highlight an area in which she had grown. My daughter replied that she had started using more spaces between words. Finally, she was asked to select a goal to work toward for next time.

"I want to try sound spelling more when writing."

This process is important for developing self-directed learners for a couple of reasons. Beyond the trust built by building on strengths together, the student is leading the assessment through thoughtful questioning by the teacher. He or she may be more likely to make improvements because areas for growth are clearly identified. By watching videoconferences with students, families can hear how they can talk to kids in a way that promotes learning. Subsequently, parents and other caregivers are more likely to emulate that language after hearing or seeing a teacher model it. In addition, by letting students know that the teacher will be checking on their progress at a later date, they are held responsible for the learning.

When my wife and I met with our daughter's teacher at the spring parent-teacher conference, one of the first things we asked was how she was doing with sound spelling.

The teacher responded, "Much better!" She then showed us a recent example as evidence. Observing how students' goals lead them to success is, unfortunately, an uncommon experience for many parents. With all of the tools available to teachers today, there is little reason why digital portfolio assessment is not being used more regularly in classrooms and schools. I attribute a lot of the growth our daughter made to her teacher's willingness to give her more responsibility in the assessment process—and to make that process more visible to us.

Reason #7: Maximize Formative Assessment

Invariably, time spent administering summative assessments means time taken away from working with students more formatively. I'm not suggesting we put a stop to all summative assessments (although the standardized tests currently in use for evaluating teachers and schools is more than questionable). Summative assessments can be a final product of a unit of study, such as a performance task to gauge whether students can transfer what they know to another context. However, what we are attempting to accomplish by embedding portfolio assessment within instruction is to maximize formative assessment and minimize summative assessment.

As already discussed, formative assessment should take place prior to summative assessment. It is the information communicated between teacher and students—and sometimes between students—that describes how well they are doing on the pathway toward success. This information, which is sometimes referred to as data, can take many forms, including classroom discussions, reading or writing conferences, feedback on various pieces of work, and self-assessments of current abilities against specific standards of excellence. In other words, formative assessment is a journey to the final destination.

W. James Popham, in his book *Transformative Assessment* (2008), offers a helpful visual that illustrates the spectrum of formative assessment inclusion in classrooms (Figure 2.1). Teachers maximize formative assessment in classrooms through carefully prepared instruction around essential understandings. The more we prepare, the more likely it will occur.

The planned aspect of formative assessment might be a shift for some teachers. That's why, in Chapter 4, the concept of backward design is addressed. This approach to curriculum and instruction gives teachers the tools to better leverage formative assessment to drive instruction.

We often associate formative assessment with basic examples, such as a "thumbs up/thumbs down" signal after a lesson. Yes, this is a form of formative assessment, but the value to the teacher is limited. When students only give a thumbs up or thumbs down to show how well they believe they understand a concept or skill, we have to ask if they truly understand the criteria for success for the given task. Are students'

Figure 2.1

Illustrative Proportions of Formative Assessment in Classrooms

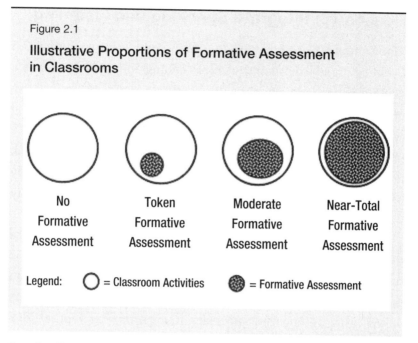

| No
Formative
Assessment | Token
Formative
Assessment | Moderate
Formative
Assessment | Near-Total
Formative
Assessment |

Legend: ◯ = Classroom Activities   ● = Formative Assessment

Source: From *Transformative Assessment* (p. 12), by W. J. Popham, 2008, Alexandria, VA: ASCD. Copyright 2008 by ASCD.

responses to this quick check a valid indicator of learning, or does it reveal an unwillingness to admit what they don't know or cannot do?

By structuring time for digital portfolio assessment in the classroom, students and teachers can have conversations that better reveal each learner's true level of understanding. There is no way for students to "fake it." They cannot game the system. Through purposeful talk and an authentic audience, teachers can capture data that are often hidden within a more basic assessment tool, such as multiple-choice questions or short-answer responses. This approach is also more valuable for future instructional plans and more meaningful to students. As a teacher, I know this is how I would prefer to spend my time.

Reason #8: Integrate Speaking and Listening

The Common Core State Standards include fewer speaking and listening standards than those for reading and writing. This is a concerning imbalance, considering that today's employers frequently prioritize prospective candidates' "soft skills," including communication and teamwork (Davidson, 2016). When I am in a position to hire new teachers or support staff, I place great stock in their ability to articulate their thinking and respond effectively to new situations. All other areas being equal, those skills usually win the position for one person over another.

Erik Palmer (2014) believes that teachers' expectations are too low when teaching speaking and listening. More of a focus will enhance our efforts in other academic areas. "Everything you do in your class would improve if students spoke better. Students would be more engaged and learn more from one another, discussions would be more productive, and groups would function more smoothly because students would be better able to express their ideas" (p. 24). There is a cumulative effect on learning when this often-neglected aspect of education is given more attention.

Using the tools that accompany digital portfolios provides a natural opportunity to embed speaking and listening skills with almost any type of performance task. For example, if students are writing original stories, then they can also be expected to record themselves reading those texts aloud and embed that audio to create a shareable audiobook. If the assignment involves a notable person from history, then students can record themselves and one another delivering that person's famous speeches or reading excerpts of that person's writing. They can then upload those recordings for families to watch and listen to online. There are so many possibilities.

The benefits of incorporating speaking and listening into the core areas of instruction are not limited to improving students' abilities to communicate. In my own observations, I have noticed how students' work tends to improve when we add this type of performance to their tasks. In the case of the audiobook example, students can play back an audio recording of themselves reading their own writing, question whether it is their best offering, and then rerecord themselves. They might also return to their texts and make revisions after realizing that the language lacked the proper prosody or enunciation when they read it aloud.

In addition to speaking and listening, digital portfolios offer more opportunities for students to convey their understanding. New and exciting tools for this work are regularly introduced to the marketplace. For example, Educreations (www.educreations.com) is a whiteboard application that allows users to create interactive screencasts. Drawings, animations, and narration can be combined to explain concepts from a student's point of view. This original content can be uploaded to or linked within almost any digital portfolio system.

This is authentic work. Future employers and organizations will expect their employees to be able to communicate effectively and listen actively to others. Speaking and listening are skills that need to be embedded within instruction today to prepare students for the future. Digital portfolios can serve as a conduit for this integration.

Reason #9: Advocate for Every Student

The use of computer-based standardized testing in the area of writing has been shown to widen the gap between students living in poverty and students who do not (Barshay, 2016). A main reason for this is the lack of familiarity with how to use a computer. Students living in poverty may not have access to the technology at home. Conversely, students from middle- and upper-class homes, on average, have more exposure to these tools. They perform better on these types of assessments versus paper-and-pencil tests.

In other words, schools with higher levels of poverty may start out at a disadvantage when using computer-based standardized tests. When we allow these circumstances to exist, we do a disservice to the very students who most need our support. So what is the answer?

One possibility is to offer an alternative for students who may not fare well on traditional tests. This can take the form of a best work portfolio: students can go back through their litany of saved work—online and off—and determine what best represents their knowledge, skills, and understandings over the course of the school year. This portfolio could follow the student's growth throughout the school years if, for example, his or her family chooses to opt out of standardized testing on an annual basis. It may be more meaningful for students in the long run—and more likely to improve their learning outcomes.

Our first priority as educators is to ensure that all of our students have access to the same high level of instruction. This is what we mean by *equity*. Schools cannot achieve equity if they do not provide every student with the same opportunity to be successful in school. Through the use of digital portfolios, students can make visible the level of success they truly experienced and how they arrived at that point.

Reason #10: Work Smarter as a Teacher

I once overheard a teacher talking about a book that her district had assigned as part of her role on an assessment committee. "It's called *Grade Harder, Not Smarter . . .*" she shared. Realizing her error, her team had a good laugh together, both at her mix-up and in the truth just under the surface of her statement.

Teachers have so many mandates and expectations from their districts, state, and school. The high level of attrition in our profession should not come as a surprise. Making matters worse, fewer individuals are going into the profession. I've personally seen this in my decade as a building principal. The amount of bureaucracy that now seems to accompany our jobs as educators is a major stressor. To retain effective teachers, what needs to give?

What students' digital portfolios can do for the teacher, given the right tools, time, and support, is an ability to collect data worth collecting. This includes actual student work, their reflections, the goals they set for the future, and the conversations they have about their growth over time. Because something is not quantified does not mean it lacks value. In some situations, limiting the translation of learning to numbers or symbols can make teaching more efficient and effective for both teachers and students. It is data-driven instruction within an authentic context.

This approach to responsive instruction may look different at various grade levels. At the elementary level, a teacher might be working on a reading strategy throughout the week. Within her students' progress portfolios, she creates an activity that highlights the goal for the week and the standard(s) it addresses. After teaching a minilesson on Monday, she uses Tuesday through Thursday to conference with students during independent reading time, which she documents through a digital conferring tool. These conversations elicit information necessary for the teacher (and student) to determine how well the skills were applied. On Friday, she has her students join her for a whole-class debriefing, using the progress portfolios to discuss the strengths and next steps she sees for the class. As an additional data point, the teacher has her students reflect on their reading in their response journals.

At the secondary level, students can be put in charge of their own curation of learning with the right amount of modeling and guidance. For example, a science teacher expects all of her students to use their personal mobile devices to curate their work from the day's lab. Students are also asked to record video of the teacher's demonstrations and audio of their group-work conversations. These artifacts provide a repository of information to review for the upcoming performance tasks. The teacher facilitates collaboration by hosting an online space, such as Google Classroom, in which all students can upload their learning artifacts for everyone in the course to see and hear. Feedback is expected and welcomed, and learning becomes a community-based activity.

The Biggest Benefit

Maybe the biggest benefit with digital portfolios for teachers is how their relationships with students change. The teacher-student dynamic transforms from a hierarchy to a partnership. We learn not only about students' academics but also about their lives, their motivations, their concerns, and their goals in life. We learn about who they are as people. This could be considered data, especially if we know how it affects learning. Yet the goals remain the same: student growth and success. It's how educators arrive at this point that we can alter our mindset about assessment.

For all of the benefits of digital portfolios, I have still observed apathy and resistance when educators try to apply more authentic assessment practices. The following three scenarios describe challenges teachers may confront in the implementation process.

Scenario #1: Your Principal Won't Allow You to Use Digital Portfolios

This is an unfortunate—yet not uncommon—circumstance for teachers. As a principal myself, I fail to understand why an administrator would not want his or her teachers to improve home-school communication and empower students to own their learning. Yet these situations do exist. The most prevalent reasons include the perceived cost for facilitating digital port-folios, concerns about student privacy, and the possibility that other teachers will also want to implement digital portfolios in their classrooms.

With regard to cost, digital portfolios can be facilitated with minimal costs to the school. Most buildings already own many mobile and stationary digital tools. With efforts by local, state, and federal organizations, reliable wireless has become a mainstay in many schools. Many students also already have the necessary technology to manage digital portfolios, including smartphones and tablets. The tools that are highlighted in the next chapter are all free to use or affordable.

Student privacy is and should be a concern for all educa-tors. It is so easy to share content—images, video, audio, text—without taking time to consider whether it should be online in the first place. This is actually another strong rationale for implement-ing digital portfolios. Consider when we take a piece of represen-tative student work and post it online for an authentic audience to view and comment on, we are modeling digital citizenship. Students see firsthand how to evaluate online content for appro-priateness and usefulness. We are demonstrating the importance of letting others see us as real people—as humans who view errors and mistakes as a necessary part of becoming better at something. This concept stands in contrast to the typical online offerings that only highlight ourselves at our best.

As for other teachers wanting to emulate what you are doing in your classroom, all I can say is, "Why not?" This is the epitome of professionalism—teachers sharing and adopting great instruc-tional ideas to improve the experiences of all students. Never-theless, there are administrators who might want to squash the spread of more authentic assessment. Reasons may include less time focused on more formal assessments, such as screeners and tests, or an inability to quantify student learning outcomes with a portfolio assessment process.

How do we handle this? My suggestion is respectfully and confidently. Teachers can make appointments with their supervisor to discuss the benefits and concerns regarding digital portfolio assessment. Be a good listener while making a case for maximizing classroom assessment that drives teaching and learning. If we've done our homework and taken a respectful approach to advocating for these practices, then it is more likely that a supervisor will also see the benefits. In fact, he or she may become your biggest champion for this approach in the future, once the inevitable success stories start to present themselves.

Scenario #2: Your Students Are Resisting Portfolio Assessment

This situation might come as a surprise, especially if you have not yet tried out digital portfolios. However, it is a common occurrence in classrooms when teachers start to engage their students in this alternative approach to assessment.

The biggest reason for this situation is because we have trained our students to be reliant on our judgment of their learning. Grades, test scores, and vague interpretations that attempt to describe their progress—such as a number of points assigned for reading a book—give few opportunities for learners to gauge their own work. Students can become overly dependent on teachers telling them how they are progressing toward essential learning outcomes that they don't know what to do when asked to be their own assessors in the classroom.

Even if students resist right away, I suggest teachers stay on this pathway. They will eventually come around. Students might need a period of "assessment detox" before we start to see success. I would begin by having a conversation with students about making this shift from teacher-directed to student-driven learning. We can start by simply asking a few questions:

- Why do schools give tests and quizzes?
- Do grades provide you, your families, and me with a good understanding of who you are as a student?

- What if teachers were no longer allowed to give scores for student work?
- How might school work in a world where numbers and symbols aren't used to assess your learning?

It's important to have an authentic discussion in your classroom about the need to shift to a better way of showing what we know and are able to do. Students' responses at every level (K–12) will be thoughtful, honest, and full of insights that we may never have considered. This activity also gives ownership to students, who now feel part of the direction that their community of learners is taking together. They will become more invested in the process because they finally have a say in it. Once students have had time to process this change in what learning looks like, I recommend starting small and leading with their strengths. Start capturing, reflecting on, sharing, and celebrating student work in an area where success has already been experienced.

Scenario #3: Your District's Mandated Curriculum Makes Digital Portfolios a Challenge

This scenario may actually be more common than a building administrator not allowing a teacher to implement digital portfolios. It's not that district leaders are directly denying the use of these connected and authentic assessment practices. When a curriculum director or superintendent sets the expectation that a certain commercial program be implemented at all grades "with fidelity," too often the program becomes the curriculum. In fact, some programs promote this as a benefit for teachers.

District leaders, legislators, and education reformers struggle to find the one tool that will address all students' needs. That's not a surprise. The one perfect model does not exist. Any program or curriculum that comes from the outside will not fit perfectly with every classroom in every school. Best practice is not exclusive to one approach. "If there were one best practice," notes education professor Mark Dziedzic, "everyone would be using that program, and education would be fixed" (personal communication). This is probably why large-scale change has been such a challenge in education. There is no one-size-fits-all solution when implementing school-level initiatives for increasing student learning. Yet districts continue to push through expensive and expansive programmatic initiatives that leave teachers and school leaders with less autonomy and fewer resources.

In these situations, teachers really have only one option—make the best with what they do have, and get creative with how to acquire what they don't. To start, teachers can take stock of available resources within their classroom and building. It might be surprising to discover what is hiding within unused spaces and storage bins. Talking to the most veteran staff members about what might be available can also be effective. For example, at my former school, I was looking to purchase some staff development resources that addressed classroom management strategies. When I mentioned this offhandedly to our special education teacher, she asked, "Have you looked in the lockers by the second grade wing?" Sure enough, an entire library of manuals and videos were stacked in multiple lockers, collecting dust.

In creating a digital portfolio assessment system, teachers should also consider the access that's already available. For example, most students at the secondary level have fairly powerful computers in their pockets, in the form of their smartphones. How can we teach them to use these mobile devices for capturing, reflecting upon, and sharing their learning? By using this technology to promote metacognition and self-assessment, we model what it means to be a learner in today's world. Students are making their work visible, which is possible within any curriculum mandate. They also see their smartphones and other digital devices as more than just a tool for communicating with peers.

At the elementary level, students need more direction and support when implementing a digital portfolio assessment process. What they do *not* necessarily need is more devices. In my previous school, we had four or five iPads in each of our K–3 classrooms. Screen time at that level should be limited. Teachers can write microgrants or request funding through websites such as www.donorschoose.org to acquire resources and devices that provide access for students. If more devices are required to upload artifacts into portfolios, consider investing in a schoolwide cart of tablets or laptops.

Linked Activity: Assessment Audit

Consider all of the assessments that take place in your classroom. List and place each assessment in one of three categories: formative, interim/benchmark, and summative. (See Figure 2.2.) Then circle the assessments that rely on quantitative (symbolic) results to reveal student information, including grades, levels, and scores.

Figure 2.2

Three Types of Assessments

Formative	Interim/Benchmark	Summative

Once completed, analyze the table. Where is most of the assessment happening in your classroom? Why? How does this affect your instruction? This visual can serve as an assessment audit and help make the case for adding digital portfolios into your instructional toolbox so you can address the needs of the whole child.

Learner Profile: Karen Fadum

Karen Fadum is a helping teacher in British Columbia, Canada, who previously taught 1st and 2nd grade. It was during her time as a classroom teacher that Karen started using digital portfolios to capture student learning and communicate it with families.

Why did you introduce digital portfolio assessment in your classroom?

I started using FreshGrade because I was approached as one of eight teachers to pilot this tool, more as a digital gradebook. The portfolio part took off, and that was not expected. After the pilot was over, I continued using it but not because of the technology—I am more about the pedagogy.

Kids are often told that they are not capable of being in charge of their own learning. But they are really powerful little beings. Portfolios started to help me have more conversations with my students. This led to how we talked about our learning and them owning it. Pretty soon, they were telling me what they wanted to document: "What I think I just built is really a good example of my number sense." The language in our classroom changed.

Once you start documenting students' pathways toward their goals, it is hard to go back to the more traditional way of doing things. After the pilot, the district offered a choice in how teachers could communicate learning with families. Many more teachers started using FreshGrade once it became an option.

Q&A **In what way(s) were the effects of implementing digital portfolios in school unique or unusual?**

My portfolio experience started with reading, both as a teacher and as a parent. Besides my classroom, watching my own children in school helped me rethink my assessment process. Knowing that each student is very different led me to believe that this type of assessment process—one that celebrated their strengths and looked at next steps—was much better for all students. Portfolios allow students to progress at their own rate instead of achieving a predetermined destination.

Allowing students to determine their own learning pathway through documentation, reflection, and goal setting helps students at all levels. We purchased iPod Touches and then taught students how to capture and upload their learning artifacts. Having these small devices for little hands allowed them to be independent with this portfolio assessment process. When they select their best work from the past month or so to upload to their digital portfolios, they are reflecting on their learning and they don't even know it.

Q&A **How would you describe the characteristics of the products from the digital portfolio work and of the educators who were involved?**

One characteristic of a successful digital implementation is that the technology needs to be easy to use yet robust enough to inform learning and future instruction. Another characteristic for successful digital implementation is working on these innovative practices as a team. If a school is known for strong learning communities and stability, it tends to be selected by district administration for trying something new. We would have been considered "edge players" since we were connected educators who had led district initiatives before and had the confidence to explore new ideas.

Q&A **What resources were used to support the use of digital portfolios?**

A change we have noticed because of this innovation is how other schools are embracing these new practices. This has been greatly helped by the district's decision to upgrade the curriculum to a more competency-based format. Students have to show what they know and are able to do. Teachers started hearing about our work and reached out for more information. In addition, the district facilitated a website hub where teachers could post questions and ideas in online communities. We could reach out together through that forum and on social media. Also, having a leader who's available to support this initiative was critical in getting the ball rolling.

Q&A **What specific outcomes do you attribute to the use of digital portfolios?**

One of the bigger changes we observed is the level of engagement boys had with books, especially at the elementary level. Allowing boys to show their learning in different ways values their learning preferences and allows them to share their understanding in different ways. This comes from the teacher knowing his or her students and using the digital tools to their advantage.

We saw a specific increase in reading confidence. Reading levels are not always accurate for younger students. When we were able to engage with them where they were and where they were going, they started to more regularly recognize their strengths—and not just in reading. For example, one of my former students who was pretty transient came to me without a lot of skills, either academically or socially. He was living with his grandmother, so she and I started a conversation about where to start. That is what we did; we highlighted that student's initial successes and shared them with home. At the end of the year, his grandmother commented about how much he grew over the year.

In your opinion, what other factors contributed to the achievement of these outcomes?

A critical factor contributing to the success of important student outcomes was the evidence-based assessment process. Kids need specific feedback about how they are doing as learners and what they need to work on for the future. Saying, "This is an *A*" does not tell them their strengths. When the teacher and student are able to show a progression of learning, starting with the learning intentions and criteria at the beginning of the year and setting the goals together, this is more effective.

Our portfolios are somewhat minimal. We are focused on quality versus quantity. How many writing samples would I need to show proficiency for this learning intention? More important, it's about how much we are involving the kids in the assessment process. How do students perceive these quizzes and checks for understanding? If it is about getting good grades, then they are not focused on learning. This has been a real shift for students who have come from a more traditional learning environment.

The curriculum needs to be strengths-based and kid-friendly. In addition, teachers need to be intentional about setting those checkpoints of when to assess learning with each student. Adding activities to the gradebook helps remind the teacher not to miss any regular portfolio conferences.

What problems did you encounter when developing or introducing digital portfolios?

A main problem is the actual technology, both in the wireless access and in the hardware. If it doesn't work, then teachers are less likely to use it during instruction. Also, there has to be a purpose to the digital tools. We have to know why we are using it. You cannot just drop off technology into the classroom and expect these innovations to happen.

Related to this is the lack of knowledge about technology in general. People might not know there is a camera on a tablet or what the term *web browser* means. What we have done that has been effective is working with other innovative educators who are ready and willing to learn how to use the digital tools. They can then guide more resistant staff to embed technology in their instruction.

What else do you think a teacher or school should know before implementing digital portfolios?

We need to have lots of conversations about promoting digital citizenship. That means, for example, whether or not we need to post images of student faces or if we can highlight the learning with them included. A question that often comes up is "Can I post a picture of students if other families are going to see?" What we have pointed out is we are celebrating our students' learning in the hallways, so doing so on the website is not a whole lot different. Taking that approach of highlighting student successes has been helpful.

Parents and families also need to be educated about the history of grades, understand student privacy policies, and have their questions answered. If they understand that teachers will be using these new digital tools with intention, they seem to be very supportive. Explaining that mistakes will be made early on also gives everyone some latitude in trying it out and learning together. These initial conversations have led to rethinking grading and possibly not using traditional assessments. It is the curriculum that drives the assessment—not the grades.

Getting Started
with Digital Portfolios

"Children must be taught how to think, not what to think."

— Margaret Mead

This chapter offers one approach for how we can introduce digital portfolios into the classroom in a manner that does not require a significant shift in classroom instruction. Beyond the technology, we are simply uploading a finished piece of student work that is accompanied by a reflection, self-assessment, and goal setting. If you have ever posted an image or a video to social media, and then added a caption or message that relates to it, then you have all the technology training you need to get started with digital portfolios.

The focus of this chapter is on highlighting work that students are already producing during the school year. Through this approach, we learn to appreciate the process of student learning along with the outcomes. Chapter 4 digs deeper into designing lessons, building a learning progression, and planning with the end in mind. In this chapter, we are looking to take that first step in integrating digital portfolios by celebrating student work in an online forum.

Develop a Yearlong Plan for Instruction

A yearlong plan of instruction is a flexible projection of concepts, knowledge, and skills to be taught and learned. This plan is broken up into discrete units of study, and each unit is generally four to eight weeks long, depending on students' developmental levels. It is not a prescriptive approach for teaching. Rather, it provides grade levels or departments with an overview of what to prepare for when teaching. In short, we are not trying to cover it all as much as we are guiding students to uncover the big ideas to be learned.

The following steps provide a roadmap for preparing instruction from September to May. This approach is adapted from a blog post written by Elizabeth Moore (2015).

Step 1: Determine the planning time and discipline for a yearlong plan for instruction.

Step 2: Bring in assessment data, including samples of student work, to identify strengths and areas for growth within the discipline of focus.

Step 3: Determine a digital portfolio tool with which to post student work.

Step 4: Schedule publishing dates on which performance tasks will be uploaded to students' digital portfolios, along with reflections, self-assessment, and goal setting.

A template for preparing a yearlong plan for instruction is provided in Appendix B. It is recommended that teachers do this work together before the school year starts. It can be especially beneficial when teachers from different grade levels or departments get together for this work. As Moore notes, "When you look at how kids in your own classroom have grown, [you can] compare with your colleagues to decide what makes sense for next year" (2015, para. 8). Housing student work in digital portfolios over time makes student growth visible for everyone involved in the learning.

Step 1

Determine the planning time and the discipline for a yearlong plan for instruction. When getting started with digital portfolios, developing a plan for instruction should start with an overview of one year's worth of teaching. This work can take place during the summer, preferably in June just after the school year has ended. Student assessment results are readily available and fresh in our mind. Getting this work completed earlier in the summer gives us the rest of our time away to recharge. We can also share out the draft with faculty and colleagues— many of whom will likely have lots of suggestions before September arrives.

The easiest way to begin the task of drafting a yearlong plan for instruction is by focusing on one discipline. My personal suggestion is to focus on literacy for this work. Reading, writing, speaking, and listening are typically the hardest areas to assess with traditional tools such as grades and scores. Integrating digital portfolios and literacy, with their ability to capture student learning in an authentic context, makes for a natural combination. If classroom time is a challenge for implementation, consider incorporating literacy with the content areas of science and/or social studies. Math and the arts also work well with digital portfolios, provided educators are not overloading students and staff with too many technology initiatives. If we try to assess everything with digital portfolios, then these tools become unwieldy and may be at risk of collapsing under their own weight.

The template for drafting a yearlong plan for instruction can be as simple or as complex as we want it to be. It all depends on the resources available and on which form of instruction is used. If a school has a selected (commercial) program, then it becomes a matter of placing the prescribed units in a preferred order, or at least outlining the scope and sequence. If a teacher or team does not use predeveloped units of study, then the process can be an opportunity to develop curriculum from the ground up.

Including students' interests and needs, along with the pride of creating robust instructional opportunities, are benefits of this approach. The challenges of building a yearlong plan for instruction in this way include the time required and a possible lack of professional resources available for this work. (See Chapter 4 for more guidance on locally developed curriculum.) Whatever approach you take, keep in mind that curriculum should closely resemble the learning that happens in real life to ensure relevance in the tasks.

Step 2

Bring in assessment data, including samples of student work, to identify strengths and areas for growth within the discipline of focus. Whether the yearlong plan for instruction is based on commercial resources or is developed locally, it should be aligned with students' strengths and needs in mind.

Standardized tests, screener scores, and benchmark data are helpful in identifying larger trends in student achievement, yet they don't allow teachers to really glean specific areas of knowledge or skills in which students might be struggling or excelling. This is important. If students are showing mastery in a certain area of instruction, why would teachers spend six weeks teaching a unit on that topic? A more cursory overview of this part of the curriculum might be all that is needed. Likewise, students who are not showing strong gains in a particular area would benefit from more instruction.

I recommend keeping in mind the following three data points when planning for yearlong instruction.

1. **Classroom Formative Assessment:** These measures of learning include checks for understanding through short-answer responses, teachers' observational notes, and anecdotal records during individual and small-group conferences.

These data drive day-to-day instruction. Housed in a digital format (preferably), they can be retrieved and studied when planning future instruction.

2. **Samples of Student Work:** This can include a variety of examples of what students produced during the school year. Though it might be time intensive to look at student work versus analyzing quantitative results, this practice guides teachers to view students beyond a score. Using this more authentic approach, "student work has become the center of education, [offering] an undistorted image of student effort and achievement" (Evans, 1993, p. 71).

3. **Teacher and Student Surveys:** How students view their learning experiences in the classroom can have a positive impact on future instruction. Teacher surveys can reveal how students feel about learning in general, whereas student surveys typically focus on a learner's disposition toward a specific discipline. As an example, Figure 3.1 shows a sample reading engagement survey for early readers (Marinak, Malloy, Gambrell, & Mazzoni, 2015).

All of this information should serve as a guide for the type of learning in which students will engage during the school year. Determining what is essential for students to know, be able to do, and feel about learning helps teachers ensure the technology integration supports the learning experience.

Step 3

Determine a digital portfolio tool with which to post student work. Once a teacher or a team has devoted time to selecting a discipline in which to integrate digital portfolios—and has evaluated students' strengths and needs in this area through assessment results—the technology for housing and sharing student work can be selected. Saving this step until we have a purpose for the tool is important. It ensures that pedagogy is a priority.

Figure 3.1

Reading Engagement Survey

My Reading Profile

Name: _____

Date: _____

Teacher: _____

What grade are you in?

1.	2.	3.
Kindergarten	First grade	Second grade

I am a _____.

1.	2.
boy	girl

Do you like to read books all by yourself?

1.	2.	3.
Yes.	It's OK.	No.

When first selecting technology for digital portfolios, teachers should determine what will best share and celebrate their students' work. If the focus is on writing, for example, will a blog or a website be the most conducive to collecting and communicating their learning? Does the technology allow for this with ease? It's also important to remember that any artifact of learning should be accompanied by reflection, self-assessment, and goal setting. In addition, consideration needs to be given to how the tool allows for students to upload and embed audio, images, and/or video, either for reflection or for the final product itself.

With that in mind, let's now look at three different types of technologies for celebrating students' best work. As already shared, performance portfolios are repositories of artifacts and reflections of students' best work. They are summative in nature and serve as a permanent digital presence of students' mastery over time. These three tools are ideal for performance portfolios:

- Blogs
- Dedicated Portfolio Applications
- Websites

They are listed in alphabetical order since the effectiveness of any one tool is dependent on the context for learning. The technology must fit the pedagogy, and pedagogy is heavily influenced by the type of learning in which students are asked to engage within their community and culture. I can't recommend one tool over another, but I can provide a description of each, along with the pros and cons of the three technologies.

Blogs

When blogs first started appearing, their original purpose was (and largely still is) to provide an online space where anyone can publish their work. Blogging was one of the first forms of digital media that allowed for two-way communication between content provider and audience. It leveled the playing field in terms of who could be considered an "expert."

Today, it's never been easier to start blogging with multiple forms of media, including video, images, and audio embedded within the text of a post. If a teacher decides to use a blog as a tool for digital portfolios, students will have the opportunity not only to collect, curate, and reflect on their schoolwork but also to engage in an authentic experience as a digital citizen. Students are forced to ask themselves, "Who might read this? Should I allow for comments? How do I promote my work with a broader audience?" These types of questions come up as students consider the authenticity of the activity and the seriousness of displaying their work for all to see.

So what does this mean for students' digital portfolios? For young students, blogging tools including Kidblog and Edublogs are good choices. For older students, Wordpress has the most robust features, is easy to use and write with, includes countless opportunities to individualize and customize one's site, and is free to use. Blogger, a Google product, is also readily used.

Blogs have features that allow users to organize their work, a prerequisite for digital portfolios.

- **Blogging:** The actual publishing that takes place happens within the writing tool of the blog. These published pieces are called posts and are the centerpiece of the blog. Writers can share their current thinking and update readers on projects.

- **Pages:** Bloggers can build as many pages as they want, along with subpages under each page. Pages can have many purposes, such as links to prior work, a short biography of the user, or a list of awards and recognitions.

- **Categories and tags:** When writing a post, users can categorize the post and add tags. Categories within the content of digital portfolios could include standards addressed or type of learning shared, such as "work in progress" or "final product." Tags are the main terms that are associated with a post. If the user posts a science report on the environment, for example, tags might include *climate change* or *life cycle.*

- **Comments:** The comments feature is usually located at the end of a post or page. The choice is up to the teacher and/or students whether they want to allow for others to comment on their posts. Benefits include providing and receiving feedback from others and developing an active audience. Challenges include depending on comments for feedback and possibly receiving negative responses (although the teacher can choose to monitor submitted comments and approve them before they appear online).

There are many more components to blogging beyond this basic list. For instance, users can monitor blog statistics to see the number of views and how many times their posts were shared on social media. These features should be reserved for more advanced blogs or for students at the secondary level. Overall, blogs might be the easiest digital portfolio for students to use in a classroom, at least when looking to get started in the process.

Dedicated Portfolio Applications

Dedicated portfolio applications are programs specifically built for documenting and sharing evidence of student growth and best work. They include multiple ways for teachers and students to capture learning and reflect on their work. For example, FreshGrade (www.freshgrade.com) is a web-based portfolio tool. FreshGrade allows teachers to upload lesson plans, link teaching resources, and select which types of assessments will be used to document and evaluate student learning. The software includes many options for the type of assessment to be used, including letter grades, total points, mastery, and anecdotal. Authentic artifacts of learning, such as video, audio, images, and text, can be uploaded from any device with an Internet connection, through either the teacher app or a web browser.

In full disclosure, we used FreshGrade in my previous school to communicate learning between home and school. We heard overwhelmingly positive responses from parents. I've also engaged in some work with FreshGrade, including writing, speaking, and training on their behalf. That said, I know that many educators utilize other tools, such as Seesaw (web.seesaw.me), for their digital portfolios. Seesaw is free to use for individual teachers. It allows students to capture their learning and share it with families through a web browser or dedicated app.

What FreshGrade, Seesaw, and other dedicated portfolio applications seem to have in common are two features. First, there is a mobile application for capturing and sharing student learning. Typically, there are different app versions for teachers, parents, and students. Notifications appear on your mobile device when a student artifact has been uploaded into the portfolio. The advantage here is how quickly family members can be informed by their smartphone or tablet. Second, these platforms do a remarkable job helping teachers monitor student mastery and growth. Apps such as FreshGrade and Seesaw give teachers choice in how learning will be measured, from traditional grades to competencies (actions and behaviors of students that are indicative of success in school).

Websites

Websites have some of the flavor of the first two portfolio tools in that students and teachers can differentiate the types of learning artifacts they display online. Learners can keep a log of their academic experiences alongside their more permanent pieces of work. I've found that the most commonly used website tool for digital portfolios is Google Sites (sites.google.com), which is also part of Google's larger G Suite for Education family of services (formerly known as Google Apps for Education). Before getting started, a template has to be selected. There is a wide range of designs among the choices offered, but students should be guided to select a relatively minimal template. This allows their work to be the focus, rather than the site itself.

Once students have selected a template, they can take one of two approaches as they get started with their digital portfolios. The first (and probably easier) approach is to create pages within Google Sites that are based on subject areas or disciplines. This might include mathematics, reading, writing, science, social studies, or any other relevant subject areas, such as physical education, art, and music. Each page is then dedicated to posting and reflecting on the artifacts selected from within that area. The second approach is to take a more specific focus on how artifacts are shared within the digital portfolio. It can be focused on the anchor standards of one discipline—say, writing. Website portfolios might also document students' pursuits of lifelong skills, such as "Design an Experiment," "Create Something Original," or "Build a Model." This is a more complex approach, yet it might offer greater rewards in the type of learning valued.

If a district uses the G Suite for Education, then it makes a lot of sense to utilize Google Sites for digital portfolios. First, students can take learning artifacts they've already developed and stored on Google Drive and embed them into appropriate pages. Slides, documents, and graphs are easy to select and insert into a dedicated Google Site. There are also other ways to document performance tasks, such as through an original video posted to YouTube or a personalized map created with Google Maps. The integration of these applications naturally lends itself to using Google Sites as a performance portfolio.

That said, Weebly (www.weebly.com) is also a powerful tool for leveraging technology to authentically assess student learning. This is the digital space that John Spencer used with his students. Weebly has much of the same functionality as Google Sites. Students can embed audio, video, images, and text within dedicated pages in their digital portfolios. For example, students can drag a photo or image right from their computer desktop into their portfolio. If your district isn't already taking advantage of the Google ecosystem, then Weebly might be an option to consider.

The biggest advantage to using a website versus a blog or dedicated portfolio application for housing digital portfolios is that it can stay with students beyond their K–12 career. Whether you use Google Sites or Weebly (or something else), students' learning artifacts and reflections have a permanent space for as long as they want. With a bit more polishing and updating, they can become professional portfolios. Using a website for portfolio assessment also gives students an immediate and positive digital footprint.

Using a website for housing students' digital portfolios is only as effective as how well teachers guide their students to select important work, reflect on their learning, and set goals for future studies. With that in mind, use the chart in Figure 3.2 to help make a decision as a school or district team about which tool is the best fit for your students, faculty, and families. There is no perfect technology here, so educators should select the tool that meets their learners' needs.

Step 4

Schedule publishing dates on which performance tasks will be uploaded to students' digital portfolios, along with reflections, self-assessment, and goal setting. This is the most straightforward part of the process. Teachers select one-week windows during which students will publish a piece of their work in their portfolios. When we put these dates on the calendar—and share the dates with students, families, and colleagues—we help ensure that we will follow through on these actions.

Publishing student work within prescribed windows during the school year can work one of two ways. One option is to allow students to select their best work from a collection of pieces. This approach might work best in the literacy classroom, such as reading/writing workshop. Janice and Calleigh provide an example of this approach at the beginning of this book. The other approach is to plan for predetermined products students will produce at the end of each unit of instruction. These performance tasks can still offer students choice and voice, such as in how they will present their knowledge and skills. All subject areas, especially those with prescribed programs, would align well with this approach. The upcoming vignette of a 3rd grade teacher, Dani, using Book Creator for a social studies project offers one example.

Figure 3.2

Portfolio Application Comparisons

Technology	Advantages	Disadvantages
Blog (e.g., Kidblog, Edublogs)	• A common tool used by many people around the world. • Allows for a wide audience to view and comment on student work. • Lends itself well to chronicling student learning, especially writing.	• Harder to organize and view learning artifacts; must use tags or categories. • Involves possibly too much visibility for students, especially younger ones. • Tools used are not readily transferrable beyond K–12.
Dedicated Portfolio Application (e.g.,Fresh-Grade, Seesaw)	• Easiest to use of all portfolio assessment tools. • Social media design engages parents via mobile devices. • Strong security measures to ensure student privacy.	• With ease of use, students may not be learning essential digital skills. • Student learning entries can become lost in all of the posts. • Dedicated portfolio applications have limited life beyond K–12.
Website (e.g., Google Sites, Weebly)	• Most relevant digital presence a student can have in the future. • Students learn the ins and outs of maintaining a digital presence. • Integration with other applications can be beneficial.	• Learning curve with maintaining a website. • Harder to communicate learning artifacts with families (versus blogs or apps). • Not necessarily built with education in mind.

Whichever approach is used, reflection, self-assessment, and goal setting is an essential part of the publishing process with digital portfolios. Without it, we are merely posting student work online. That's great for communicating with families, but it probably won't make an impact on student learning. It is helpful to have protocols for this type of work. Protocols help streamline the assessment process and allow students and teachers to focus on the work and themselves as learners. I developed one protocol, OWN (Observe, Wonder, and Next Steps), as a way to complete this work (Figure 3.3). Each step corresponds with

Figure 3.3
OWN Protocol

Observe: Take a step back from the work, and notice and name qualities of student work.

Possible prompts for *reflection*:
- Why are you including this piece in your portfolio?
- What makes it stand out among your body of work?
- To what extent does this work best represent your understanding?

Goals: affirmation and celebration

Wonder: Take a closer look at student work with a constructive and critical eye.

Possible prompts for *self-assessment*:
- What might a friend or classmate say about this work?
- How does this work compare to the previous pieces you included?
- If you had to change one part of this piece, what would it be? Why?

Goals: self-critique and deeper understanding

Next Steps: Take a look forward in order to build on current knowledge, and set goals for the future.

Possible prompts for *goal setting*:
- In what area(s) do want to improve?
- How will you grow as a learner?
- What do you need to continue learning in this area?

Goals: habit building and appreciation for lifelong learning reflection, self-assessment, and goal setting, respectively. The metacognition facilitated through the OWN protocol is critical for making this a deeper learning experience. We value the process of learning—and so do students.

Janice and Calleigh's conference followed this process somewhat. Younger students are going to need more modeling and guidance with reflection, self-assessment, and goal setting. Shared demonstrations, with one student sitting with the teacher in front of the class as they conduct a public conference, is an effective way to model this process. By contrast, older students should be able to take the reins of this process. They can have access to this protocol and respond to it through audio, video, or in writing to provide context for the associated piece of work. It bears repeating: all students should be submitting some form of reflection, self-assessment, and/or goal setting that is attached to the work being uploaded. It can be in any media, but should give context and meaning to the work students are sharing.

Figure 3.4 illustrates a general progression a classroom may take in terms of releasing the responsibility of who is facilitating the reflection, self-assessment, and goal setting during a portfolio assessment window. There is no right way to do this. The goal is on guiding students to achieve independence.

Four Shifts to Anticipate
When Implementing Digital Portfolios

As educators get started with this work, it is worth noting that this is a change in how we do business. Many teachers say they are "doing" digital portfolios, but more often than not, they are merely capturing and sharing student activities with families online. There's nothing wrong with this, but we also shouldn't kid ourselves into thinking that this is portfolio assessment. A teacher should experience some level of challenge with implementing digital portfolios in their classrooms. With that, the next

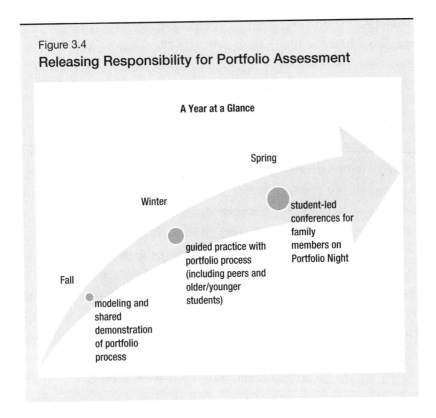

Figure 3.4
Releasing Responsibility for Portfolio Assessment

A Year at a Glance

Spring

Winter

student-led
conferences for
family
members on
Portfolio Night

guided practice with
portfolio process
(including peers and
older/younger
students)

Fall

modeling and
shared
demonstration
of portfolio
process

part explores four shifts to anticipate when implementing digital portfolios within the classroom.

Shift #1: Making Mistakes Publicly

Using technology in classrooms is challenging enough on its own. Mobile devices demand a strong wireless connection, long battery life, and properly working hardware and software. Highlighting student learning via digital portfolios raises the expectations for using technology, at least if it is done with intention. The assessment process is not as easy as taking a weekly trip to the computer lab and having students play an online game or respond to a prompt on their blogs.

When we throw more variables into the teaching equation, mistakes are bound to happen. This is not a judgment of the quality of teaching. Rather, the capacities of today's technology have yet to meet the expectations and demands of today's classroom. It will get there. In the meantime, teachers should be ready for things to not always go as we might hope.

Having a solid lesson plan when modeling technology use for students is critical. Specifically, it's important to have a list of steps for creating digital content and a plan for capturing and communicating this learning online. Having these procedures in place helps teachers mentally prepare and anticipate any problems in the process. Developing a comprehensive lesson plan when first introducing technology to students also gives teachers the opportunity to identify how they will gradually release responsibility for the activity to students.

Regie Routman (in press) offers a helpful visual, called The Optimal Learning Model (Figure 3.5), for teachers to guide students to become independent learners and thinkers.

As noted, teachers should start with modeling and then quickly bring in students to help demonstrate the work. In addition, teachers should be encouraged to have a backup plan if the technology goes awry. For example, reflection can be taught with or without technology. Educators should not let the digital tools get in the way of the learning outcomes. It should be conveyed to students that mistakes will happen, and that is okay. Learning without errors isn't really learning anyway.

Eventually, those who are most involved in the process—teachers and students—have to be active participants. They should be the leaders of their own learning.

Example of Practice: Modeling Technology in the Classroom. Dani, a 3rd grade teacher, wants her students to go beyond the traditional informational report for their world geography unit. Their past performance tasks were fine, yet they did not align with how information is conveyed in the 21st century. Specifically, audio, video, and images are primary tools for communicating information in today's connected world. As such, Dani

Figure 3.5
The Optimal Learning Model

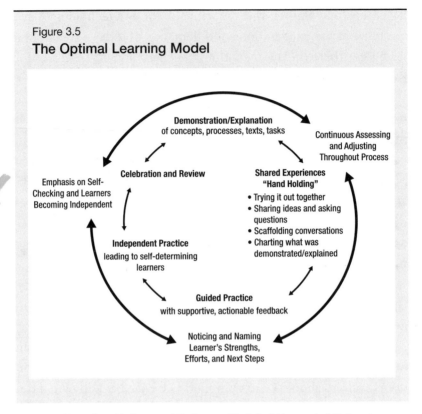

Source: From *Literacy Essentials: Engagement, Excellence, and Equity for ALL Learners,* by R. Routman, in press. Copyright © 2017 by Stenhouse. Used with permission.

feels that her students are ready to incorporate these types of media with their informational reports.

With advice from a colleague, she decides to use Book Creator (http://bookcreator.com/) for this performance task. Book Creator is an application that allows students to create digital books that include images, drawings, audio, and text. These texts can then be uploaded to YouTube, exported into iBooks, or saved as a PDF file if audio is not necessary.

Dani has access to a cart of iPads for this work. She takes one of the iPads home with her to try creating a multimedia text. This time devoted to using the technology helps her develop a comprehensive lesson plan (Figure 3.6). Dani also incorporates student

Figure 3.6
Book Creator Lesson Plan

Daily Lesson Plan

Teacher: Dani   School: Howard Elementary   Date: 1/17/17

Lesson: Introducing Book Creator   **Grade:** 3   **Time:** 1 hour

Objectives: To understand tools available for creating original digital content for world geography report.

Skills: (from 1d: ISTE Student Standards)
- Understand the fundamental concepts of technology operations.
- Demonstrate the ability to choose, use, and troubleshoot current technologies.
- Transfer knowledge to explore emerging technologies.

Materials: iPad; Book Creator app; Reflector mirroring app

Instructions:
1. Explain that students will create an original digital book about a country of their choice using Book Creator.
2. Display iPad screen on whiteboard, and model for students how to open up Book Creator and use basic tools.
3. Pair up students and distribute iPads for partners to explore.
4. After a short time exploring, have a student come up to front. Together, develop a short story that incorporates all four types of media (image, audio, drawing, and text).
5. Have partners work together to create their own original story.
6. At the end of the lesson, have a few groups mirror their iPads to share their stories with the class.

Evaluation: By the end of the lesson, all students should be able to create an original story that incorporates all four types of media.

standards from the International Society of Technology in Education (ISTE). The standards are designed to empower student voice and ensure that learning is a student-driven process (2017).

To ensure that she gives students an opportunity to take the lead in this learning, Dani allocates the majority of her lesson plan time to have students explore this tool. During the beginning of the lesson, however, the technology that allows her to mirror her iPad screen to the projector and whiteboard doesn't work. Fortunately, Dani has confidence in using the tool and doesn't panic. After realizing that she needs to have her iPad on the same wireless frequency as the mirroring software, her iPad screen pops up on the whiteboard. Students are involved in the activity throughout the lesson, thanks to the shared demonstration and guided practice. The assessment at the end of the lesson gives Dani concrete evidence of whether her students are ready for the next step of the project.

Shift #2: Changing How We Teach

No amount of technology will affect student learning and achievement unless teachers change their practice. In fact, the introduction of technology into a classroom not currently experiencing success with student learning might actually make things worse. According to a survey at my prior school, we experienced only small improvements in student learning outcomes. Classrooms were using technology largely for consumption, with few opportunities for students to create original content. This was despite an abundance of available digital devices, including tablets and laptops.

When implementing digital portfolios and related technologies, we should expect complex work. What seems like a simple act—documenting and reflecting on student learning over time—introduces more variables into the teaching equation than we might anticipate. For example, when we record a student reading aloud and reflecting on his or her own writing, what are we now unable to do as a teacher? The use of digital tools to capture and share our best work and progress over time changes what we prioritize as teachers. There is only so much time in the school day. Maybe what gets cast by the wayside should have happened sooner. For instance, some worksheets and low-cognitive-level activities would be pushed out of instructional time.

These instructional changes may also influence the physical design of the classroom. If authentic practices such as multimedia creations and digital portfolios become a major part of this process, how we as teachers set up the learning space needs to allow for this to take place. For example, a teacher could create a portfolio booth, in which students can scan a QR code to call up their digital portfolio application on a tablet and take a picture of their finished work. The teacher would also expect students to write or record a reflection and self-assessment of their final product as they upload the image to their digital portfolio. He or she would provide an assessment protocol at the booth.

Example of Practice: Developing a Rubric with Students. In Dani's 3rd grade classroom, pairs of students are busy collecting information about a country they selected from a choice of four. They are using both print and online resources to engage in this research. As Dani walks around observing her students, she notices that information being gathered is pretty basic: population, the country's flag, and location on a map are the most common.

She wants her students to go deeper. By understanding other cultures, we come to understand our own a little bit better. This results in an increased appreciation for the world in which we live—a critical competency for globally connected citizens. Dani decides to guide students in developing a rubric that reflects this deeper understanding about their chosen countries. Using the essential questions of the unit—"What can we learn about other countries and cultures?" and "Why is understanding our global neighbors important?"—she and her students brainstorm a list of criteria for an excellent digital book (Figure 3.7).

This process takes longer than just handing students a premade, teacher-designed rubric. Time spent codeveloping the expectations means less time for other classroom activities. However, the conversation they have about the expectations is lively and smart. For example, when Dani asks the class, "When

Figure 3.7

Book Creator Rubric

Student's Name: _____ Teacher's Name: _____

Country Report/Digital Book

	Advanced	Proficient	Basic	Minimal	Notes:
Content					
Information is accurate and based on multiple sources.	☐	☐	☐	☐	
Information is interesting.	☐	☐	☐	☐	
Details help audience appreciate culture.	☐	☐	☐	☐	
Digital book helps audience better understand home country.	☐	☐	☐	☐	
Digital Integration					
Audio, images, drawings, and text are included.	☐	☐	☐	☐	
Original music from country is incorporated.	☐	☐	☐	☐	
Audience can interact with text (e.g., press audio button to play narration).	☐	☐	☐	☐	
Delivery					
Students clearly explain process for developing digital book.	☐	☐	☐	☐	
Audio, images, and drawings support understanding of text.	☐	☐	☐	☐	
Digital book is accessible for a variety of audiences.	☐	☐	☐	☐	
Students understand benefits of using multimedia with writing.	☐	☐	☐	☐	

you state, 'The information is interesting,' what do you mean by *interesting*?" Students offer a variety of responses:

- "It makes me want to read more about the country."
- "Because I read that book, I might want to visit that place."
- "The book made me laugh; I had fun reading it."

"Is that okay?" Dani thinks aloud. "Should reading an informational text be fun?" They consider some of the nonfiction books they read consistently. A number of them take an unusual, sometimes even humorous, stance to a piece of history or geography. For example, the *You Wouldn't Want to Be a . . .* series provides information about people and cultures from our past through the hardships they encountered and why we are fortunate to be alive in today's world. With this knowledge in mind, the class decides to keep *interesting* in the rubric but flesh it out with specific indicators. Dani also makes a mental note to bring more high-interest informative texts in the classroom so students can continue to immerse themselves in the genre. A goal is for students to translate this genre of reading to their digital writing.

Shift #3: Handing Over More Responsibility to Students

Digital portfolios provide a better way not only to document and share student learning but also to own it. Like a stamp or baseball card collection, kids can and will ruminate over what they have curated with a specific purpose. What students keep, what they discard, and what they want to showcase to the world—and why—are at the heart of portfolio assessment. Teachers should provide the time, resources, and guidance for students to engage in this deep process in order to become more self-directed learners.

As students start to become the lead assessors of their own learning, we release a part of a role that has long resided with the teacher. This is not an easy process. Whether we feel like students won't learn without our direction or that the classroom will become a bit messier than we are used to, these feelings are warranted. Our practices are personal; we are who we become in education.

The benefits of releasing to students more of the responsibility of assessment outweighs the costs. Students become invested in the outcomes of their own learning and take pride in the journey they took to get to a point of success. When they start to own their learning, they are more motivated to do it right and to do it well. This typically leads to increased achievement. Once we witness the joy that students and families experience when they are engaged in portfolio assessment with digital tools, the shift feels worth it.

Example of Practice: Showcasing Student Work in Digital Portfolios. Students have already storyboarded their writing and found images related to their country of choice. They are now ready to pull this all together as a digital text within Book Creator. Dani hands out the iPads and lets them go. She walks around the classroom, quietly noticing the pairs at work. Because they developed the rubric together and discussed as a class what a successful project might resemble, Dani is pleased to find that she doesn't need to remind her students to avoid spending too much time on the nonessential aspects of what Book Creator has to offer.

In a few situations, students have to be encouraged to do the best they can and not worry too much about making it perfect. One pair is trying to capture the best audio narration possible. They record their voices for one page of text, play it back, decide it's not to their satisfaction, delete the recording, and try again. After the fourth try, Dani directs the two students to look back at the rubric they created together: *How important is the audio recording to the entire project?* After a short reflection through discussion, they decide to move forward.

After a couple class periods working on this project, students are feeling good about the digital books they are creating. Once they agree that the project is ready for publication, Dani helps each pair upload their work to YouTube. This allows their books to be "watched" along with their narration, images, drawings, and text. The YouTube link is then pasted into the students' digital portfolios where they add reflection, self-assessment, and goal setting to their linked work. Their parents receive a notification on their smartphones or tablets to view the content at their leisure.

Shift #4: Working More Collaboratively with Colleagues

We cannot expect to change assessment practices and then not subsequently change instruction. When the definition of *success* takes on a new meaning, and students are no longer defined solely by a test score or grade, multiple avenues toward excellence are also created. Our job as a teacher transforms into a knowledgeable, student-centered coach who can guide each student toward collaboratively determined goals along a more personalized pathway.

As these changes in practice become visible for students, they also become visible to our colleagues. They start to notice the difference—especially in their conversations with students, peers, and parents.

"Did you see the project we finished in class?" says a student.

"I was impressed with how the students did on this task and their enthusiasm for posting it online," comments a teacher.

"Wow, I love how I can see my son's work in real time!" shares a parent.

Responses by colleagues usually fall into one of two camps: concern or interest. The concerned colleague—one who questions the use of digital portfolios with students—might be a manifestation of the school's current culture. The phrase "That is not how we've done things in the past" reflects the beliefs of a teacher who does not value risk taking or innovation. It reveals an aversion to anything different. This type of educator values the status quo, which is a safe place to be but rarely benefits students. Seeking better practices is a threat to this type of educator. The best response to concerned colleagues is to listen, thank them for expressing their thinking, and continue to engage in this authentic form of assessment for students. Continued comments that discourage innovation should be directed to the building principal, who should be supportive and protective of this important work.

Conversely, interested colleagues seek understanding. They see the enthusiasm displayed by students, their family members, and the innovative teacher—and they want to learn more. These educators embody the concept of professionalism: one who continuously seeks better ways to improve their practice, because it is about the student. Teachers need to connect with these colleagues and engage in common assessment practices. Working in isolation—without a coalition of support—while developing digital portfolios can pose problems. Through this collective work, teams of teachers can redefine the culture of a building as an institution of learning.

Working more collaboratively with colleagues also provides accountability. When we change the way we teach, there is a period of time when what we're doing doesn't feel natural or comfortable. The temptation to revert to simpler practices is strong. That is why having a team involved in the process is important. Portfolio windows are set with colleagues for uploading, reflecting, and sharing student work. Dates are selected in which said work will be discussed with teams to find patterns and trends regarding students' strengths and areas for growth. Having this positive peer pressure makes the implementation of portfolio assessment a more likely reality.

Example of Practice: Collaborating on an Integrated Unit of Study. The country project now completed, Dani can't help but share the results with another grade-level teacher.

"I've never seen the students more engaged in their work! They were so diligent about creating the best digital book for this unit. I don't know if it was using Book Creator as a way for them to represent their learning, or if it was knowing that their work would be shared online with their families through their digital portfolios. Maybe it was both? The families left lots of positive comments on their work in their portfolios." The other teacher is already aware of the project, having brought her students in to watch Dani's students present their projects. She has been supportive of her work the entire time.

The music teacher, John, overhears their conversation. His interest is piqued by Dani's enthusiasm, and John informs her that he is looking for better ways to incorporate culturally diverse music in his classroom.

"Next year, what if we collaborate on this world geography project? The music they learn would connect with the four countries they research." Excited about the connections students could make between social studies and music, they agree to move forward with this plan. In their combined approach, students would still present reports to their classmates and upload them into their digital portfolios, but John would also upload video of students performing dance demonstrations representative of their countries. Authentic instruments and accurate language would be incorporated into their performances. Ultimately, students and families could experience documentation of this connected learning experience all in one digital space.

Conclusion

With digital portfolios in the classroom, the outcomes of instruction become more than just an end-of-the-unit test. Teaching becomes more cyclical and responsive when the essential understandings, questions, and tasks are made clear. Coverage is replaced with deep understanding. You see the data you collect as information for your current and future planning, instead of simply documenting a score in the grade book. This type of work is the starting point for students to become the primary assessors of their own learning.

Linked Activity: Rethinking Classroom Design

Designing a classroom with both students and their learning needs in mind takes imagination, creativity, and a sense of advocacy. If you are not sure what's "right," then imagine your own child, grandchild, niece, or nephew in the classroom. That's my litmus test whenever I supervise learning in a school. Consider the following steps to rethink your learning space.

1. Visualize what your classroom looks like at the moment. On a separate piece of paper, draw it as well as you can.

2. Now imagine what you would need to change to allow for digital portfolio assessment to take off in your classroom. Consider your own yearlong plan for instruction along with the following issues:

   • Access to technology.

   • Different methods of instructional delivery.

   • Available resources and what is still needed.

   • Opportunities for teacher-student partnerships and peer collaboration.

   • Developmental needs of students.

   • Space to allow students to reflect on their work.

3. Sketch how your classroom might need to change to accommodate this new way of assessing and learning. Ask students to offer their ideas for what's possible. Don't worry about costs or permission at this time. Just create what you and your students want to see.

Learner Profile: Lisa Snider

Lisa Snider is a high school journalism teacher/adviser in Duncan, Oklahoma. She teaches digital communications and introductory journalism, and serves as adviser for student publications.

Why did you introduce digital portfolio assessment in your classroom?

It all started with a conversation I had with my personal learning network, or PLN. Specifically, I joined the Teachers Throwing Out Grades Facebook group, facilitated by Mark Barnes and Starr Sackstein. I learned a lot about the importance of student reflection and teaching them how to collect their personal work for assessment. In the past, I had students blog, but we needed a more private space for their works in progress before publishing.

I also learned through my connections, reflections, and experience that no one tool works for everyone. As I implemented a portfolio assessment process, I discovered that it was important to put part of this process for selecting tools in the students' hands.

 In what way(s) were the effects of implementing digital portfolios in school unique or unusual?

Portfolios, especially when utilized through digital tools, gave me another way as a teacher to assess students' levels of understanding. What a score couldn't tell me, often the actual student learning artifact could. I had to model this process a couple of times for the students. Some kids caught on right away, while others needed more support, which was fine.

As digital portfolios became a part of my regular practice, I started using strong portfolio examples of past and present students for my instruction. In terms of the tool, WordPress is what we use for publishing our posts in the digital communications classes. In my intro to journalism class, we keep a Google Drive folder of students' works-in-progress. With Google Drive, students share their work with me and I offer feedback. The work kept in that folder is more of a progress portfolio versus the performance portfolio the digicomm students use with WordPress.

 How would you describe the characteristics of the products from the digital portfolio work and of the educators who were involved?

At this time, I am the only teacher using digital portfolios in my school. Also, I do not assign grades but ask students to decide what grade they feel they earned. They make their case to me, using artifacts they produced during the school year to support their position.

What resources were used to support the use of digital portfolios?

My classroom is the journalism lab. It has 12 iMacs and 4 MacBooks for the publications staff to produce the newspaper and yearbook. If I have classes with more students than equipment, we have to be flexible.

What specific outcomes do you attribute to the use of digital portfolios?

Reflection has been a key to student success. When I ask students to justify the grade they feel they earned, they have to pore through all of their past work they have put together and published. They look at the entire process and reread work samples of their writing. What they come to realize is that they have had control of the outcomes (and their grades) the entire time.

In your opinion, what other factors contributed to the achievement of these outcomes?

Providing time for students to redo their work or seek help is important. Kids learn at different rates. At the same time, not having any type of deadline is also a problem. I am constantly tweaking this part of my practice and trying to make it better for me and for the students.

What problems did you encounter when developing or introducing digital portfolios?

One problem has been the lack of support for my new approach in assessing student learning. I have permission to explore this type of work, such as self-assigning grades, but I have not heard any positives or received any feedback. Permission is not the same as support.

Also, technology can always be an issue. Students will often want to take home their work and finish it, so I let them check out one of our MacBook Pros. Unfortunately, they may not have wireless at home, so they have to find a public location to work. Also, and this is a surprise, some students are still confused about Google Drive and how more than one person can work on a document.

What else do you think a teacher or school should know before implementing digital portfolios?

As teachers, we need to be connected in online spaces. There is so much support from other educators through social media. I regularly visit Facebook groups, such as Teachers Throwing Out Grades. Twitter is also a great source of information. I follow #jerdchat (journalism nerds) and engage in their chats about this subject in education.

We have to be willing to share our own work and thoughts online, through blogging and other publishing tools. Admit mistakes publicly and discuss solutions you tried. Most important, find other educators who share your same passions for digital portfolios and other topics of interest.

Digging Deeper
into Digital Portfolios

"If you don't understand yourself, you don't understand anybody else."

—Nikki Giovanni

If a teacher were to stop at Chapter 3—and be content with that level of digital portfolio work—he or she would likely find positive results. Students will feel more involved in the assessment process, and families will appreciate knowing how their children are doing during the school year. There may even be larger gains in your students' achievement levels. I've experienced these results, including a 19 percent increase in students' writing abilities from fall to spring after implementing digital portfolios in our writing curriculum (Renwick, 2016). This was almost double what we previously saw with respect to writing growth.

However, there is more potential in leveraging technology not only to showcase student work but also to document learning growth and reflection. Capturing the more formative pieces of evidence that informs teaching and learning through digital tools can elevate instruction to new levels. In this chapter, we explore how technology can be used to facilitate progress and process portfolios to support student learning and outcomes. Designing instruction with the end in mind helps facilitate this successful technology integration.

Three Types of Portfolios

We've already learned about the following three types of portfolios:

- **Performance portfolios** are collections of a student's best work, with the student taking the lead in the selection of the work and providing an explanation for why they should be included.
- **Process portfolios** contain several versions of a selected work. Such a portfolio might hold early drafts of a paper or poem to show how the piece developed over time.
- **Progress portfolios** are often managed by teachers. They hold collections of work intended to illustrate children's development over time.

It should be noted that process portfolios in the context of digital tools may also help reveal student thinking during longer learning experiences, such as maintaining an online journal via a blog during a project. Using any one of these approaches to authentic assessment would likely yield better student learning. So why try to incorporate multiple digital portfolios into instruction? How might these different approaches work in concert? What would be the cumulative effect of a multifaceted approach to digital portfolios?

Why incorporate multiple digital portfolio approaches into instruction? Showcasing student work six to eight times a year in a discipline of choice, along with reflection, self-assessment, and goal setting, is a formidable practice. Yet we still wonder: Where did the journey for this student's work begin? What trials did he or she experience? What successes did he or she celebrate to get to excellence?

People live through stories. They are their own protagonists in their personal endeavors. Using digital portfolios to capture student growth gives context to their best work. They start to attend to the processes they used to achieve success. This builds lifelong learners because students learn how to learn. The veil is lifted for everyone involved on how students arrived at essential learning outcomes.

How might the different approaches work in concert? To get some context for this question, let's go back to the initial examples from Chapter 1. If you recall, Barry is a high school language arts teacher. He found his students' writing lacked both skill and voice, so he made the decision to use technology not only to increase his students' writing skills but also to give them more ownership in their work. For example, students were taught how to create folders for their writing projects within Google Drive. Barry showed them how to organize their writing based on what was published and what was still a work in progress.

Because the classroom has access to one cart of Chromebooks, every student can access their writing and projects as needed. They can check out the Chromebooks if they want to continue working on a piece at home. Barry demonstrated how to separate their published pieces in one folder and their works in progress in another. He also recommended never throwing away a piece of writing that didn't work. He tells students, "They might be useful to you down the road, either as a revised stand-alone piece or as part of a new piece." Students are taught how to share their unpublished drafts with peers and how to provide feedback for each other both in person and online.

The performance portfolio is the published work in the folder and on Google Sites. The process portfolio includes those comments and suggestions made by the teacher and peers before the work was published. These pieces of evidence should be documented in (or at least inform) the reflection, self-assessment, and goal setting of the published piece as commentary. The progress portfolios rest in Barry's hands, possibly through a digital conferring tool that also leverages Google. For example, he might utilize a template created in Google Docs or Google Forms to document where each student is at in his or her writing projects, along with a list of minilessons he might teach in the future based on the feedback he gets when conferring with students.

While the level of independence will change with students' age and abilities, using multiple digital portfolios for authentic assessment helps students connect their growth as a learner with learning itself. It moves the assessment work from "the teacher assigned it so I have to turn it in" to an ongoing process of starting, drafting, getting feedback, revising, and eventually publishing authentic work in real contexts. It is a comprehensive approach to digital portfolio assessment, where one part of the work directly supports the other two (Figure 4.1).

What would be the cumulative effect of a multifaceted approach to digital portfolios? The answer to this is generally one of two things: a highly responsive approach to instruction, or a big mess.

Why a mess? Because we are asking ourselves as teachers not only to have students upload artifacts of finished work online with commentary but also to maintain works in progress (a process portfolio) while we also keep our own digital files of student growth (a progress portfolio). These are a lot of plates to keep spinning at the same time. Capturing formative assessment is critical for informing today's instruction. Yet expecting to do this well without more support may serve to be too much of a challenge for any teacher.

To facilitate a multifaceted approach to digital portfolios that ensures highly responsive instruction, developing curriculum with the end in mind—or backward design—can be effective.

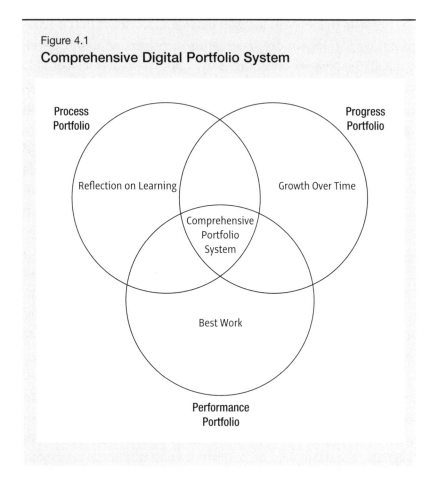

Figure 4.1
Comprehensive Digital Portfolio System

Backward Design

This concept for curriculum development is the basis for almost all contemporary instructional design methodologies, including Understanding by Design (Wiggins & McTighe, 2005) and Project-Based Learning (Larmer, Mergendoller, & Boss, 2015). Planning instruction with the end in mind follows three essential steps:

1. Identify desired results.
2. Determine acceptable evidence.
3. Plan learning experiences and instruction.

Because this book is focused on digital portfolios in the class-room, we'll take a more basic approach to curriculum development. Readers are encouraged to explore more formal methods of instructional design, described in the resources already shared. Figure 4.2 shows a template that can be used for basic curriculum development with the integration of digital portfolios.

Using backward design to integrate digital portfolios in the classroom has several benefits. First, by identifying the big goals for a unit of instruction, teachers ensure that teaching and learning are the priority. Technology is secondary. Second, the possibilities for performance tasks with digital tools expand greatly. Students can utilize and combine audio, images, video, and text to create a unique representation of their understanding that is not possible without technology. Finally, the access to digital tools to capture formative assessment results can make developing the learning progression a more student-centered experience that honors their best way of showing what they know and can do.

Another advantage of basic backward design (versus a more formal curriculum development approach) is that the plans are more accessible to students and teachers. Instruction that integrates digital portfolios should be written using classroom-friendly language. For example, a basic draft of a unit of study is presented to students from the beginning. Dialogue and questions follow, which inform the pathway toward excellence as the unit progresses. There is a fluidity to the process. Students are partners in the learning trajectory, including how they will be assessed with progress and/or process portfolios. Nothing is determined for sure before students begin engaging in instruction. This naturally leads to the curriculum becoming more relevant and meaningful, which should lead to higher levels of learning made evident through a performance task shared online in a performance portfolio.

As an example, Cathy from Chapter 1 adopted CCPensieve as her digital conferring tool. She uses this application when meeting with her 1st grade students about their reading growth. This

Figure 4.2

Backward Design Template

#1: Identify Desired Results	#3: Plan Learning Experiences and Instruction	#2: Determine Acceptable Evidence
Theme/Concept:	Entry Event:	Summative Assessment:
Standard(s):	Learning Target: Learning Experience: Formative Assessment:	"As a _____ (role), _____ (verb) . . ."
Big Questions:	Learning Target: Learning Experience: Formative Assessment:	Expert Understanding:
Big Ideas:	Learning Target: Learning Experience: Formative Assessment:	Amateur Understanding:
Vocabulary:	Learning Target: Learning Experience: Formative Assessment:	
Resources:	Learning Target: Learning Experience: Formative Assessment:	Media for Performance Task: ☐ Audio ☐ Video ☐ Image ☐ Text

progress portfolio facilitates goal setting developed through the teacher and student and is based on current assessment data. As the year progresses, Cathy realizes that students need opportunities to show what they know independently and to monitor their own growth as readers.

Cathy decides to formally introduce digital portfolios to her classroom in order to provide this purpose and audience. She signs up for Seesaw and creates an account for each student. Cathy uses the gradual release of responsibility/Optimal Learning Model (Routman, in press) to teach students how to reflect on their reading within the blog feature of Seesaw. She selects this tool because of the access it provides for younger students to draw, type, or upload digital media and express their thinking and themselves as readers. Cathy also shows students how to post a blog to their permanent portfolios and how their work will serve as an artifact of their learning that should be celebrated.

As Cathy continues to confer with students after introducing Seesaw, she notices a greater sense of purpose in their reading. One student asks, "Can I post a review of the book I read on Seesaw?" Cathy begins to understand how audience affects purpose in student learning experiences, given the appropriate level and amount of digital access. She starts thinking with the end in mind and planning for authentic products and projects that students can complete to showcase their literacy knowledge and skills.

Next, we explore the three stages of backward design and how digital portfolios might be integrated.

Stage #1: Identify Desired Results

To determine what is essential for students to know and be able to do, educators almost need a crystal ball. Jobs that are here today may be gone tomorrow. Likewise, occupations that do not exist now may be popular—even essential—by the time our students graduate. This is why schools need to think beyond the Common Core State Standards and consider what is "lifeworthy" for a dynamic future. The concept of lifeworthy learning comes from David Perkins's work at Harvard's Graduate School of Education. In his book *Future Wise: Educating Our Children for a Changing World* (2014), Perkins asks a big question: "What did you learn during your first twelve years of education that matters in your life today?" (p. 10). This wondering segues into Perkins defining lifeworthy learning in six different ways:

- Beyond basic skills: 21st century skills and dispositions.
- Beyond the traditional disciplines: renewed, hybrid, and less familiar disciplines.
- Beyond discrete disciplines: interdisciplinary topics and problems.
- Beyond regional perspectives: global perspectives, problems, and studies.
- Beyond mastering content: ability to think about the world with the content.
- Beyond prescribed content: much more choice of what to learn.

This shift in focus on what it means to be "educated" or "literate" in the world calls for different approaches to teaching and learning. The Common Core State Standards, even though they provide more clarity about expected student outcomes, do not adequately address the needs for a changing world. Digital portfolios, with their ability to house and share artifacts of learning that convey many ways of being smart, allow for this shift. The first step in identifying lifeworthy learning is looking at standards beyond the Common Core that consider what else students may need to know and be able to do.

- **ISTE Student Standards** (www.iste.org/standards/standards/for-students-2016): The standards created by the International Society for Technology in Education (ISTE) address several lifeworthy tenets for a more modern educational experience, including being a digital citizen, knowledge constructor, innovative designer, and creative communicator.

Much of the media that people consume and create today exists online in various multimedia formats. It therefore makes sense to give our students these experiences before they graduate.

- **Partnership for 21st Century Learning Framework** (www. p21.org/our-work/p21-framework): There are common threads that run between ISTE's standards and this framework. The Partnership for 21st Century Learning is most well-known for its focus on the four Cs: critical thinking, communication, collaboration, and creativity. This framework was developed in partnership between the educational and business worlds. The goal is to create a better alignment between what schools are teaching and what employers are looking for.
- **Habits of Mind** (www.habitsofmindinstitute.org): The founders of this framework, Art Costa and Bena Kallick, have discovered and developed 16 dispositions that learners exemplify in their pursuit of knowledge and truth. These habits include persisting, managing impulsivity, questioning and problem posing, and finding humor. Their vision with this work is to "create a more thoughtful, cooperative, compassionate generation of people who skillfully work to resolve social, environmental, economic and political problems" (Institute for Habits of Mind, n.d., para. 2).

In reviewing these different expectations, a few things stand out. First, students are asked to be creative producers of new information. For example, they aren't merely asked to write a persuasive essay; they should also be able to identify the media that will best persuade a specific audience and then pursue that project. This requires knowledge about both the medium and the message. Second, and this follows from the first point, students are positioned as problem finders, instead of only problem solvers. With current frameworks for curriculum and instruction, students may be limited to a few options to demonstrate their understanding. Student voice and choice should exist within each option for a performance task. Finally, these indicators for what it means to be a learner in the 21st century are hard—maybe even impossible—to capture with traditional assessment tools. This alone makes a strong case for implementing digital portfolios in the classroom.

What the desired results look like in the context of a unit of study depends largely on the discipline and grade level. An example of the desired results, from Lori's middle school mathematics example in Chapter 1, is provided. The unit of study is "Bridges," a project-based unit of study in which students apply principles of three-dimensional geometry to an authentic problem (see Figure 4.3).

The integration of a 21st century learning skill, a habit of mind, and a CCSS writing standard demands a different way to document students' understanding in the summative assessment. Technology supports the performance task.

Stage #2: Determine Acceptable Evidence

There should be a tight weave between what students are expected to know and be able to do and how the summative assessment will allow students to showcase their understanding. One of the most important parts of any summative assessment is ensuring that the performance task is authentic. Students should be engaged in real work for an actual audience. Even if the task students are asked to do is engineered by the teacher, it should closely resemble the learning and work that would happen beyond the classroom. We want students to almost forget they are in school when they are engaged in their work.

One way to ensure authenticity is by having students role-play actual occupations such as scientist, mathematician, author, blogger, website developer, reporter, engineer, environmentalist, or any other occupation that appropriately connects to the focus of the unit. Wiggins and McTighe (2005) have pioneered this

Figure 4.3
Identify Desired Results

Theme/Concept: Bridges

Standards:
- *Mathematics:* Solve real-world and mathematical problems involving area, surface area, and volume. (CCSS.MATH.CONTENT.6.G.A.1, A.2, A.3, A.4)
- *21st Century Skills:* Communication and collaboration
- *Habits of Mind:* Persistence
- *Writing:* Write arguments focused on discipline-specific content. (CCSS.ELA-LITERACY.WHST.6-8.1)

Big Questions:
- How are bridges built?
- When were the first bridges developed?
- What different types of bridges are there?
- How do engineers decide on the type of bridge to be built?
- Why do we need to know geometry?
- When are bridges necessary?

Big Ideas:
- Bridges connect people from one land mass to another.
- Purposes for and styles of bridges change over time.
- Bridges depend on sound mathematical principles.
- Bridges can serve as a metaphor for relationships.

Vocabulary:
area, perimeter, angle, vertices, surfaces, polygon, coordinate plane, parallelogram, triangle, trapezoid, communication, collaboration, persistence, opinion, persuasion

approach to performance tasks. The role should also be complemented by an authentic task that addresses several criteria and reveals student understanding at a deep level.

- The task should require students to transfer what they learned to a new situation.
- The task should reveal what each student knows and is able to do, even if it involves working with partners or in teams.

- The task should focus on deep understanding of the big ideas described in the unit.
- The task should have a specific description for what excellence looks and sounds like.

Of all the criteria, the most important is that there is a close alignment between the goals and objectives of the unit of study and the summative assessment (performance task). The other criteria support and deepen the work students are asked to do.

Assessing performance tasks can be a challenge. Because they are embedded in authentic work, a paper-and-pencil test alone is not going to suffice because there is no transfer, although a traditional summative assessment could be used as an additional piece of evidence. This is why digital portfolios work so well with performance tasks. Student learning conveyed in writing, audio, images, and/or video provides an unfiltered look at what students know and can do. It is learning made real.

There are three technologies—screencasting, podcasting, and video creation—that work well for a variety of such performance tasks. Keep in mind, though, that the digital tools should serve the purpose and audience for the learning. Access to these tools without intent is a mindless integration of technology.

Screencasting

Screencasts are captured media that contain audio and video of a presenter's annotations and animations. They can also be narrated and presented on a desktop computer or mobile device. Screencasting is often used to provide educational tutorials. They came into prominence when Salman Khan made his online lessons public through YouTube and then Khan Academy. Using nothing more than a digital scribing tool and an audio recorder, he provided original online tutorials in mathematics for a relative, which branched out into almost every academic area. Today, education uses screencasts in Khan Academy fashion as a way for students to teach one another the skills and knowledge they desire. Next are three tools that are up for this task.

- **Educreations** (www.educreations.com): If you are looking for an easy way for students to share their knowledge and ideas with others—both locally and globally—then this tool should be considered. Educreations allows users to record their drawings, images, text, and voice, save it online, and then share their final products with others. Educreations can be an opportunity for students to assess their classmates not only on what they learned but also on how they delivered the content. Speaking and listening become an integral part of the performance task. For students who struggle with this part of school, technology can provide a necessary scaffold. Teachers have also found this tool to be helpful in delivering lessons to students when they are away from school. The substitute teacher receives the link to the screencast, presses play, and the lesson commences. In addition, Educreations can be an essential resource in a blended learning environment where students return to a specific lesson to review the content.

- **Explain Everything** (https://explaineverything.com): Like Educreations, this screencasting tool allows users to visually convey information in an engaging manner. What Explain Everything has over Educreations are several bells and whistles. For instance, with a site license, multiple users can collaborate on a single project, adding images, drawings, text, and audio to develop a presentation. The ability to work with others in a digital environment is an essential skill in today's world. Explain Everything also works intuitively with many storage and file sharing platforms available online. If your students are ready for a robust tool when completing a performance task, this whiteboard application would be a wise choice.

- **Screencast-O-Matic** (https://screencast-o-matic.com): When the task does not demand a high level of production value—say, in a quick tutorial on how to use a computer application—then Screencast-O-Matic might be the best tool. I use this one frequently when there is a request by professional colleagues for a step-by-step approach to navigate the features of online software. Teachers can return to various screencasts, saved to YouTube, as many times as they need. These quick and easy screencasts can also have a place in a performance task. For example, students who are providing basic tutorials for community members on how to use a computer can use Screencast-O-Matic to develop those tutorials. Students will learn the importance of brevity, clear directions, and content developed with a specific audience in mind.

Multiple performance task ideas can be incorporated with screencasting:

- Create math tutorials for peers.
- Explain a complex science concept.
- Post a book trailer.
- Communicate directions to school visitors.
- Teach younger students school expectations.

Podcasting

Podcasting is captured audio that is accessible online. Files can be housed on digital devices or streamed directly from the Internet. Podcasting might be simple in theory, but the power of this medium should not be underestimated. (I speak in terms of audio-only podcasts; there are also video podcasts.) Podcasters can easily attach introductory music and a summary of the content. That's all that is necessary to produce an episode. It's also why podcasting is an excellent tool for allowing students to convey their knowledge about a topic of study.

In small groups, students could summarize content to create a script. They rehearse their show, listen to their audio recording on a mobile device, make revisions, and then create their podcast. Podcasting might provide the easiest access for students and teachers who are considering embedding digital tools within their performance tasks. The limitations of an audio-only environment can benefit the learning by spurring creativity and innovation in how students can communicate their understandings and skills to an authentic audience. That they can upload their final products to the world only makes these types of tasks that much more purposeful.

- **audioBoom** (https://audioboom.com): If you are looking for the easiest experience in creating podcasts, this may be the tool for you. audioBoom does one thing really well—it records your audio and posts it online. This is the essence of a podcast. What I appreciate about this type of technology is the limitations it brings to students. They cannot get too fancy with the fonts or transitions between slides like they might with written reports or slide presentastions. The focus is on producing a high-quality presentation that represents student learning. All of the extraneous details fall by the wayside.
- **GarageBand** (www.apple.com/mac/garageband): This program is almost like having a recording studio on your mobile device. Students can record their audio and play it back to assess their performance. What differentiates this technology from audioBoom is the robust set of creative tools available. For example, after recording audio of a conversation, students can layer in music they produced within GarageBand. This includes keyboard, guitar, percussion, bass, and string instruments. They can even plug in an instrument to record their own music and create a track. Once everything is ready, students can upload their finished product to SoundCloud, iTunes, audioBoom, or other services that publish audio files online.

- **Skype** (www.skype.com/en): For creating podcasts with participants from across the country and around the world, Skype is it. At first glance, you might not associate this tool with podcasting. When we Skype someone, we generally think of having a video chat with that person. What I've discovered is that many professional podcasters prefer Skype for facilitating conversations for their podcasts. The sound is clearer, especially when speaking with someone in another location. With the help of third-party applications, Skype can capture audio and save it for later use as a podcast. It is quite impressive technology. Of these tools, Skype is the only one that works on any platform.

Multiple performance task ideas can be incorporated with podcasting:

- Broadcast an investigative report.
- Document a field trip.
- Record an interview with an important subject.
- Create book reviews.
- Develop advertisements for local businesses.

Video Creation

Video creation offers the broadest opportunities for integrated media: video, audio, text, and narration all within one tool. There are many sensible connections between educational video production and how it is used in the world today, including commercials, documentaries, and newscasts. Even though kids are watching less television does not mean they have slowed down their media consumption. YouTube, for example, has become the go-to media source for many kids, and smartphones and tablets are becoming the primary access point. It makes sense to tap into students' interests when developing performance tasks through the use of video.

One note of caution when allowing students to use technology for performance tasks: students may engage too much in the bells and whistles when using these digital tools. It's fine to let them play with the technology to better understand it, yet teachers only have so much time during the school day. This is a reason why units of study should be developed ahead of time. Educators should ensure that the performance task is closely aligned with the standards, goals, and essential understandings for instruction. Criteria can be developed that highlight student expectations during a performance task. Teachers should make sure that expectations are clear from the outset.

The following three tools are recommended for this type of activity, depending on the hardware that is available in your school.

- **iMovie** (www.apple.com/imovie): When it comes to video production, there is iMovie and there is everything else. No other piece of software comes close to matching the benefits that this application offers. Users have a choice between developing an informative movie with videos, photos, and music, or they can create a trailer that follows a Hollywood-style movie trailer template. An informative movie would be useful for summarizing content learned during a history unit or for documenting change over time as it relates to a scientific concept. Students might make trailers to develop a commercial for a book they read or a product they developed. They could also apply persuasive writing with this format in order to advocate for a community cause or make a special request to the school principal. One of iMovie's best features is how all of the media a student has captured can be saved across multiple devices (multiple Apple devices via iCloud). The editing tools in iMovie are also easy to learn and teach. Completed videos can be uploaded to YouTube or watched on an Apple device.

- **Camtasia** (www.techsmith.com/video-editor.html): Camtasia began as a screencasting tool but developed into a formidable video studio. For schools that have access to Windows products, Camtasia is a sensible choice. Like iMovie, Camtasia offers users a landing page to import different forms of media, along with an editing bar to organize and create informative, narrative, or persuasive content. Eric Marcos, a middle school mathematics teacher, routinely asks his students to create video tutorials for their peers about essential understandings from the curriculum. Marcos notes the importance of peer explanations and the impact they have on student learning: "Maybe some students just like that it's a kid who's explaining it, and it makes them think, 'Oh, I should be able to handle this and understand it too; it's no big deal'" (November, 2012, p. 29).

- **TouchCast** (www.touchcast.com): If access to digital hardware is more limited, TouchCast might be your answer. It is available both through the web and as an app. TouchCast provides users with many templates for newscasts and video reports. One of the best features is the greenscreen technology. Purchase a greenscreen cloth, hang it up in the classroom, find an appropriate image for the background, and students can record themselves "delivering the news" from anywhere around the globe. This makes TouchCast a go-to application when students want to create reports about a geographical location or a specific time in history. All they need is an appropriate and relevant image and they're ready to go. Also worth noting is the interactive nature of the videos produced with TouchCast. Students can create questions that appear during the video, which allows the viewer to answer and provide feedback. Social media feeds and digital maps are also available to showcase while students' presentations are playing. TouchCast offers a vision for the future of video creation.

Multiple performance task ideas can be incorporated with video creation:

- Produce a public service announcement for a nonprofit organization.
- Write and publish a digital story.
- Create an end-of-the-year montage.
- Communicate information with global peers to broaden perspectives.
- Pose a question to crowdsource ideas.

To summarize, performance tasks need to be tightly aligned with the desired results to ensure that students can truly transfer knowledge, skills, and dispositions to a novel situation. How technology is selected for students to communicate their understanding should be an intentional process. If the digital tools are a distraction to the performance tasks, teachers are better off sticking to more concrete summative assessments. Even these can be documented with the features of a digital portfolio tool, such as a speech, presentation, or similar demonstration. In addition, any performance task should be accompanied with a written explanation and reflection of the work. This gives the teacher an additional source of information to gauge the level of students' understanding.

Figure 4.4 is an example of what Lori's performance task might resemble for the bridge project she assigned to her math students. She elected to stick with one standard of excellence and not offer students to strive for only an amateur understanding of three-dimensional geometry.

The presentation could certainly be a screencast that is accompanied with a written report. Getting too specific in these directions might leave students feeling like the project was a contrived task. Class discussions can be facilitated regarding the technology that would best serve the purpose for learning. Considerations include the best way to communicate students'

Figure 4.4

Determine Acceptable Evidence

Summative Assessment:
As a team of engineers, design a proposal for building a bridge over a local body of water. This proposal should include digital renderings of the bridge and a physical prototype that incorporates the major concepts learned in our geometry unit. The team should also create a multimedia presentation that persuades the city council to go forward with your plan.

Standards of Excellence:
- Prototype for bridge incorporates major concepts of three-dimensional geometry.
- Blueprints for bridge incorporate major concepts of two-dimensional geometry.
- Presentation leverages persuasive writing strategies and multimedia.
- Students share their thinking about their team's process and progress, especially related to persistence and collaboration, in a growth digital portfolio.

Tool for Performance Task: Explain Everything
- ☑ Audio
- ☑ Video
- ☐ Image
- ☑ Text

findings with an authentic audience and the level of participation students might want from posting their bridge proposals online. Regardless, the performance task should allow the teacher to capture students' work in a digital format that elicits information about student understanding.

Stage #3: Plan Learning Experiences and Instruction

If the essential outcomes and performance tasks of a unit of study describe the destination, then the learning progression is the journey students take to get there. The planned learning experiences and instruction should identify the smaller, incremental steps that should lead to deeper understandings. In other curriculum frameworks, there can be coding or matrices involved to help ensure alignment between standards and lessons. Although these can help teachers feel assured that they are "covering" the standards, this format may not be very student- or teacher-friendly. The goal with planning learning experiences at the classroom level is to unpack the standards and performance tasks into teachable lessons that address the necessary knowledge and skills.

The purpose for planning learning experiences within the work of building a pathway to success is to scaffold student experiences by creating learning objectives and to check for understanding with formative assessment.

Create Learning Objectives

To develop a learning progression that leads students to essential outcomes, the standards and expectations need to be broken down into manageable lessons. The learning objectives of these lessons need to describe the outcomes that the lesson is designed to produce. These objectives comprise the day-to-day classroom instruction.

There are two critical parts for a successful learning objective: (1) what students are asked to do, and (2) the learning action. The focus for instruction should revolve around learning as an active process and not a passive activity. For example, instead of stating, "Students will practice drawing squares, triangles, and circles," a teacher would write, "Students will compare squares, triangles, and circles." The first objective is focused on an activity and is not measurable. The second objective is focused on learning and can be assessed. Using digital tools to authentically assess student growth and achievement requires learning to occur.

When writing learning objectives, the verbs should be active and at an appropriate level of thinking. Active verbs describe what students will specifically do to attain knowledge or a skill.

Examples of active and specific verbs include *define, explain,* and *evaluate* (as opposed to more passive verbs, such as *understand, know,* and *appreciate*). The verb within the learning objective should also describe the thinking involved for the learning experience. Lower-cognition verbs include *list* and *identify*; higher-cognition verbs include *analyze* and *create*. See Figure 4.5 for an example of how the specificity and complexity can be increased in objectives. Some of these ideas derive from the book *Where Great Teaching Begins* by Anne Reeves (2011).

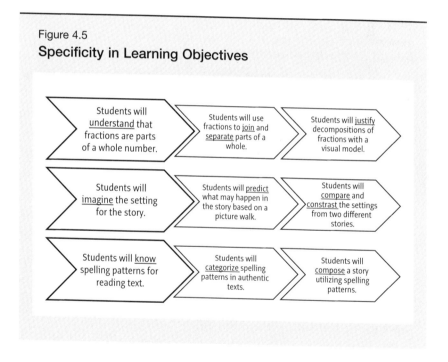

Figure 4.5
Specificity in Learning Objectives

Students will <u>understand</u> that fractions are parts of a whole number. → Students will use fractions to <u>join</u> and <u>separate</u> parts of a whole. → Students will <u>justify</u> decompositions of fractions with a visual model.

Students will <u>imagine</u> the setting for the story. → Students will <u>predict</u> what may happen in the story based on a picture walk. → Students will <u>compare</u> and <u>constrast</u> the settings from two different stories.

Students will <u>know</u> spelling patterns for reading text. → Students will <u>categorize</u> spelling patterns in authentic texts. → Students will <u>compose</u> a story utilizing spelling patterns.

The learning that is to occur and the verbs used to convey this action often come directly from the standards used. Consider this 7th grade English Language Arts standard from the Common Core State Standards:

Determine two or more central ideas in a text and analyze their development over the course of the text; provide an objective summary of the text. (CCSS.ELA-Literacy.RI.7.2)

As you can see, there is a lot to learn here. Unpacking this standard into more manageable objectives, it might look like this:

- Determine two or more central ideas in a text.
- Analyze development of central ideas over the course of a text.
- Write a summary to synthesize ideas of a text.

Notice that the level of thinking increases with each objective. Students are asked to do more complex tasks as they engage more deeply in the learning. This is what teachers want to see as they guide students to understand the big ideas of a unit.

Design Formative Assessments

In a unit of study, every learning objective should have a formative assessment assigned to it to check for student understanding. The results should be used to inform future instruction and respond effectively to student needs.

There are two general types of formative assessments: classroom and common. Classroom formative assessments are the day-to-day and even minute-to-minute interactions with students, and they usually occur as teaching is happening. Typical classroom formative assessments include student questioning, observation of student dialogue, and informal conferences. The Optimal Learning Model is dependent on this type of assessment for moving students toward independence. Classroom formative assessment is tailored to meet the needs of the individual.

For our purposes in using progress and process portfolios, we focus on common formative assessments, which are developed around the most important learning objectives. What makes these formative assessments "common" is that they are administered to every student in the classroom or across classrooms within a grade or department. They can include multiple choice, constructed response, or performance tasks. What makes them powerful is the close alignment between the assessment and the objective. This helps ensure that the results from a common formative assessment are reliable for adjusting instruction.

The goal in using any formative assessment is to elicit feedback about a student's current knowledge or skill level. This feedback can be provided by the teacher, or it could come from the student looking at his or her own work with an understanding of the criteria for success. Regardless of the source, the most important aspect of any form of feedback is that it helps the learner move forward and improve.

Facilitate Formative Assessment with Digital Portfolios

There is some reluctance in creating a digital portfolio dichotomy in which there is only a progress portfolio or a process portfolio. That said, having a structure for administering formative assessments to measure growth over time (progress) and how students grow (process) is helpful for teachers when they are in the middle of classroom instruction. Consider the following digital tools for managing this work.

Progress Portfolio Tools

- **CCPensieve:** This conferring tool gives teachers a digital platform to focus on one of four reading strategies during independent reading: comprehension, accuracy, fluency, or vocabulary. The teacher and student together decide on goals around one of these four strategies. Anecdotal notes and other qualitative information can be documented within CCPensieve. This software also has the capacity to keep track of progress in writing, mathematics, and other content areas.
- **FreshGrade:** This digital tool, already discussed as a dedicated portfolio application, has a robust assessment feature for measuring student learning progress. Teachers can enter learning objectives, connect them to standards, and determine the appropriate assessment for each task. When teachers enter results into FreshGrade, the software

provides a visual representation of which students are above, at, and below proficiency for flexible grouping.

Process Portfolio Tools

- **Google Drive:** Using these free tools gives students a digital space to house their work. Work can be organized based on what stage they are at in the learning process. When students are ready, they can publish their best work directly from their Drive accounts to a Google Site. The integration among all of Google's programs makes it an effective tool for documenting the learning process over time.
- **Kidblog:** Blogging as a way of communicating current thinking for an authentic audience has been effective for quite some time. Because it is so closely related with word processing, blogging can simplify the transition from a static to a dynamic approach to documenting learning. Kidblog offers a safe platform for students to share their thinking and receive comments from peers.

Figure 4.6 shows Lori's progression of learning objectives, learning experiences, and formative assessments for the geometry unit of study. The digital tools, such as FreshGrade and KidBlog, are included within the formative assessments to best capture evidence of student learning. The objectives listed have specific verbs that are actionable and assessable. As the learning experiences are presented, students are asked to participate in more complex tasks as they get closer to the performance task. This is how scaffolded plans can work to ensure students can successfully transfer knowledge to a new situation.

Linked Activity: Develop a Unit of Study

Use the template provided to develop curriculum that integrates multiple digital portfolios. Get plans down on paper or digitally, and then try it in the classroom. The goal is not

Figure 4.6

Plan Learning Experiences and Instruction

Entry Event
Watch video of Tacoma Bridge and read *The New York Times* article on 2007 bridge collapse in Minneapolis.

Learning Target
Find area and perimeter of various two-dimensional shapes.

> **Learning Experience**
> Lessons from mathematics textbook
>
> **Formative Assessment**
> Constructed-response quiz, documented in FreshGrade

Learning Target
Find area and perimeter of various three-dimensional shapes.

> **Learning Experience**
> Lessons from mathematics textbook
>
> **Formative Assessment**
> Constructed-response quiz, documented in FreshGrade

Learning Target
Compare and contrast different bridge types and purposes.

> **Learning Experience**
> Acquire knowledge about bridges from identified websites.
>
> **Formative Assessment**
> Multiple-choice quiz on essential understandings regarding bridges and application of geometry.

Learning Target
Draw and develop two- and three-dimensional shapes to design an acceptable proposal for a bridge project.

> **Learning Experience**
> Create designs and prototypes for suggested bridge.
>
> **Formative Assessment**
> Post designs in FreshGrade, self-assess work.

(continued)

Figure 4.6
Plan Learning Experiences and Instruction (*continued*)

Learning Target
Communicate and collaborate on a team focused on creating a proposal for building a bridge in the local community.

Learning Experience
Work as a team member on the bridge design project.

Formative Assessment
Daily blog posts on Kidblog about the process for developing a bridge-building project.

perfection but action. The feedback you receive from your students will inform future instruction, even during the unit of study itself. If you feel the need to get feedback from other educators, please share your work in our Digital Portfolios Google+ Community at http://bit.ly/dspinaction.

Learner Profile: Margaret Simon

Margaret Simon is a gifted and talented education specialist in New Iberia, Louisiana. She works with many students in several schools, specifically related to English Language Arts. Margaret is a strong proponent for student blogging and has highlighted many benefits she has found in her work. Notably, blogging

- Opens the doors of the classroom to the world.
- Gives students an authentic voice.
- Encourages writing to become an everyday activity.

- Feeds and nourishes students through the commenting and feedback process.
- Provides automatic portfolios and student mentor texts at your fingertips.

Why did you introduce digital portfolio assessment in your classroom?

I first introduced digital portfolios because I teach the same students year to year. It is an academic pull-out from their classroom. Through Kidblog, our process portfolio tool of choice, I can follow students' progress from when they enter the program until they exit the school (6th grade). Often, I am assigned students without any information regarding their writing abilities. That is why we use Kidblog. Once, when I went to ask a teacher for a writing sample for one student, the teacher mentioned that she never seems to get to the writing part. This was disappointing for me to hear, yet it did not deter me from getting this student started in regular writing habits. When I started working with this student, it was like a door was opened. She started blogging at least once a day.

In what way(s) were the effects of implementing digital portfolios in school unique or unusual?

Blogging is a focus for the program; it's individualized for that student. All of the students from the other schools I work with are blogging together. They have readers who comment on their work as a real audience—peers at different grade levels and abilities. Gifted and talented students sometimes lack opportunities to connect with peers at their current cognitive level. To model this process, I also blog and help facilitate deep connections between students and other educators and writers. For example, I have a student in 6th grade and have had her since 1st grade. She is a very good poet who lost her mother too soon. I wrote about her mother's death when she was in 4th grade. Amy Ludwig VanDerwater, a poet, saw this post and connected with the student via email. They communicated with each other quite a bit, exchanging poetry. Amy ended up sending the student some of her published books.

 How would you describe the characteristics of the products from the digital portfolio work and of the educators who were involved?

This sense of audience is a big driver in motivating students to write online frequently and make their process as writers visible. We've had other authors, such as Sharon Creech, Kate Messner, and Cynthia Lord, visit kids' blogs. I've sent out their posts with the author included on Twitter to get their attention—authors whom I feel would be good connections. These connections with an authentic audience have benefited me directly. The relationship that developed between Amy Ludwig VanDerwater and my student has enhanced my practice. For example, Amy was working on an educational resource about poetry. She asked me for samples of my students' work to highlight. In addition, I often feature my students' work on my blog so they have a wider audience. With this approach, the line between school and real world is often blurry.

Each Tuesday, my students engage in Slice of Life. This initiative comes from the blog Two Writing Teachers (www. twowritingteachers.org). Each week, students are challenged to write about what's going on in their lives. It is an exchange of stories from and between classrooms. Students connect with peers through Kidblog who are also doing the Slice of Life challenge. With permissions in place, kids can see a stream of peer bloggers who are also participating in this activity. They are expected to leave constructive comments on other students' blogs from all across the United States.

 What resources were used to support the use of digital portfolios?

Regarding resources, my students do not have 1:1 access to computers. Instead, they have a rotation system of who gets a computer on certain days. For celebrating student work, they have Promethean boards to project a piece of student writing, notice what's good and needs work, and use the student's writing as a model. Once it is on the student's blog, I do not have nearly as many papers. Print resources are also a mainstay in my practice, including titles from Amy Buckner, Ralph Fletcher, Georgia Heard, Katherine Bomer, and all of the connections available online. In addition, I use Voxer a lot (a walkie-talkie-like app). We meet as a small group of writing friends and just talk with one another about what we are doing. This is really nice, as I live in a smaller community, so I get the opportunity to communicate within a teaching network via social media such as Twitter and Voxer.

 What specific outcomes do you attribute to the use of digital portfolios?

Not every student in our gifted and talented program is a natural writer. Motivation and persistence are not uncommon challenges. For a while, documenting word count has been something I was resistant to. However, the previous year (during the Slice of Life challenge), another gifted teacher's students were producing amazing work. I asked, "How do you get these kids to write so much?" She shared that she tracks word count. Now I require a word count minimum of 250 words. Students have met my expectations and then some. They will even compete with themselves, pushing themselves to write as much as they can. One student who was barely writing 100 words is now writing 400 words at a time. The word count forces them to elaborate on their writing and dig deeper into their work.

 In your opinion, what other factors contributed to the achievement of these outcomes?

One of the best outcomes of blogging through the Slice of Life initiative and other blogging opportunities is that my students no longer fear writing. It's comfortable for them. I require three blog posts a week: Slice of Life, Wonder Wednesday, and a reader's response. Just that practice, that daily writing, is critical. I have to remind my students that blogging is writing, just like using paper and a pencil. Some of my students, especially boys, have a harder time coming back to handwriting after blogging for a while. With gifted students, and really all students, their opinion is not a trivial matter in their minds. When they participate in writing digitally for an audience, their thoughts are important. What they share makes a difference. It's empowering to them. Writing online goes beyond just what we are teaching them. It builds them up as a person.

What problems did you encounter when developing or introducing digital portfolios?

My students would not always have access at home. That is why I usually do not require them to complete a blog post beyond school. When I do expect some work from home, a few come up with excuses. Some of my students without a home wireless connection will find ways to access the Internet, such as at the public library. The conditions are changing, just not very quickly. Another issue is that many students' parents are not yet attuned to this new way of writing. They think, "Oh, my kids are on the computers and they are just playing games and stuff." They haven't quite come to the understanding that students writing online is something important. The parents are sometimes not letting their kids on. They get nervous about letting them on the Internet or having a phone.

What else do you think a teacher or school should know before implementing digital portfolios?

Teachers should not be afraid of the technology and allowing students to have access to that technology. There is a lot of misunderstanding about the safety of blogging. Kidblog is a very safe space for students to write online. There isn't any hacking or inappropriate comments. Some teachers are hesitant to give students that freedom. However, we have to provide for them the opportunities to take risks in a safe environment.

That is something that I have learned in this process. For example, an older student blogged about some friendship troubles she was having. Another student read this and shared it with peers. This led to the class having a heart-to-heart conversation about the situation. In reflection, there was a lot of learning that came from this experience. We can provide that safety net so students can apply their skills and learn from their errors.

5

Going Schoolwide
with Digital Portfolios

"The single most important thing you could do tomorrow for little or no money is have every student establish a digital portfolio where they collect their best work as evidence of their skills, where they're working with their teachers and other adults to present their best work, to iterate their best work, so that they actually have real progress they can show."

—Dr. Tony Wagner

Leadership Is Essential

In this chapter, we change the audience to focus on school leaders. The importance of understanding the tenets of a school-wide approach to implementing digital portfolios cannot be overstated. By "school leader," I mean not only the principal but also instructional coaches, technology coordinators, curriculum directors, superintendents, and teacher leaders.

Many educators with whom I spoke in preparation for this book were leading on their own, or—at most—had the support of a small team of colleagues. Although their work was making a visible impact on their students, I wondered about the other students in their respective schools who did not have access to those practices and processes. Inequity is fostered when there is a lack of agreement about what better practice is and looks like.

One of the best benefits of going schoolwide with digital student portfolios is the coherence that is developed when all teachers are on the same page. If each grade level or department is facilitating the portfolio assessment process with fidelity, then all students should have access to equally high levels of instruction. The focus of educators resets from what is taught to what is learned, and results have more of a priority than before. Equity can become a reality.

As teachers and students consistently engage in the portfolio assessment process, I have found that the culture of learning changes with it. When we place value on our students as learners and mistake makers, the journey is celebrated along with the destination. Our collective understanding of the role of assessment expands beyond grades and test scores. As David Niguidula (2010) notes, "The process of teaching is about far more than checking standards off a list or 'getting through' a curriculum. It's about getting to know students as individuals and as groups; it's about recognizing that Olivia's interest in science fiction lights up her interest in writing or that Mario's skill at assembling (and disassembling) indicates that he prefers hands-on experiments" (p. 153). A school becomes a true learning community when this shift in priorities happens.

I have advocated for multiple practices and possibilities educators can adopt in their approach to authentic formative and summative assessment. However, let me be clear about the steps in going schoolwide with digital student portfolios. Without principal and superintendent support, it will not happen. You can count on change stagnating in unsupported situations. In this chapter, I share specific steps school leaders can take to make this change a reality.

Going Schoolwide

Getting to a point where teachers needs minimal support in integrating technology into their classroom instruction takes time and persistence. Teaching and learning are incredibly complex processes on their own. Throwing technology into the mix can further complicate things if the necessary pieces are not in place to make it work. School leaders need to bear in mind that adding technology to the school day should be preceded by addressing outstanding issues regarding curriculum, instruction, and assessment.

Integrating portfolio assessment within teaching and learning will have its challenges even when the academics of a school are strong. Necessary integration steps include looking at your school's assessments and level of access, having interested teachers start the process on a small scale, and developing a purpose for digital portfolios that goes beyond merely being connected. The purpose for this type of initiative should be about improving and transforming current educational practices. An initiative such as this should not be an attempt to close an existing instructional gap but rather an effort to support a current school initiative.

Even with a strong instructional system in place, there will need to be a lot of modeling, shared demonstrations, and guidance to ensure that the technology is used to its full potential. Leaders should consider instituting the training as schoolwide professional development; otherwise, some teachers might dismiss the initiative as just "one more thing to do." That is why it is imperative that leaders understand the purpose exactly and how it will positively affect student learning. Professional development that connects back to a bigger purpose for the work helps the parts connect with the whole.

Let's explore some strategies a school leader can take for successfully going schoolwide with digital portfolios.

Start with Assessments

By starting with assessments, we place value on what we measure. People identify priorities through leaders' actions more than their words. This means taking the focus off standardized testing and reframing our perspectives on day-to-day learning interactions. It's not that we are ignoring our state and district mandates; we are instead choosing to shine a light on a different part of the assessment spectrum.

When we engage in a conversation about the many types of assessments used in school, invariably someone will associate the word *assessment* with high-stakes testing and grades. People are quick to generalize this concept. It helps as a leader to have a conversation with faculty about the rich array of possible ways to assess student learning and get students more involved in the process. As discussed throughout this book, teachers can use audio recordings, anecdotal notes, observations of group conversations, pictures, video, self-assessments, daily journal entries, short-answer written responses, and exit tickets as powerful assessment pieces. Any of these options would serve students well within a progress, process, or performance portfolio, depending on the context.

Where the leader comes into the process is when he or she acknowledges that there is a problem with how assessments are currently being used. We have so many ways we can measure students about their achievement. Yet how many of these can be used to drive our work and inform our instruction? If they are summative, are we celebrating each student's accomplishments, or merely documenting results we pretty much knew would be the outcome all along? These questions can lead to authentic conversations about finding balance in our students' learning lives and developing ways for everyone to recognize their impact. This is an opportunity to revisit basic concepts about assessment literacy, such as the difference between formative and summative assessments, and reinforce the importance that almost all assessments can be formative if we use them in way that informs instruction.

To begin, a school leader can start expecting qualitative learning results to be assessed and submitted periodically. For example, teachers can collect and analyze writing samples at selected intervals throughout the year.

Assess Your Level of Readiness

There are few things more frustrating than when a teacher is trying to teach a lesson and the technology fails. Maybe the wireless signal is not strong enough for uploading multimedia content, or there are not enough devices for students to document their learning at the same time. Whatever the situation, making sure that the technology is working is imperative to the success of any digital initiative.

I have experienced this firsthand. In our initial forays into digital portfolios, I asked all teachers to try out an application with our newly acquired iPads. Unfortunately, the application was not designed for K–12 students (it was for professional artists). Subsequently, teachers struggled to document student learning and upload it for an authentic audience. This led to a lot of frustration and an eventual cancellation of our first attempts at using digital portfolios in the classroom.

To help leaders assess their school's readiness for a technology integration initiative, a basic checklist is located in Appendix A. It can help school leaders reflect on the level of access and gauge the purpose and audience needed to successfully implement digital portfolios. I recommend completing this checklist as an instructional leadership team to ensure that many perspectives are considered and staff feel like they have input into the process.

Once the digital portfolio readiness results are available, they can be shared with the faculty. Starting with what is going well and then moving into areas that require more growth helps ensure feedback is heard. At some point, a decision will need to be made about how the school wants to proceed. It's important to start small in order to develop buy-in and to test out new tools and ideas. However, if a school is ready to move forward with adopting technology in a thoughtful and meaningful way, then there is no reason to wait. Working with technology specialists to help facilitate this assessment is critical for success.

Start Small

This point cannot be overstated. Leaders have to be patient and allow change to move forward organically, preferably with teachers in the lead. Otherwise, it can be seen as a top-down initiative. Positive outcomes are worth the wait.

Right now, I am living out my beliefs. I am a relatively new principal in my current school district. After 16 years in one organization, it was time to move toward different opportunities. Within a few months of getting hired, a couple of teachers were already inquiring about using digital portfolios. They were interested in trying out two specific tools to see what worked best for them and their students. I was all for that.

This desire to adopt technology immediately is tempting. I am just as susceptible as anyone. However, until we can identify a purpose for the digital integration, these initiatives often fall flat. By posing the following three questions in this particular order, the focus likely remains on student learning:

1. Why do we want to use digital portfolios with students?
2. How might this look in our classroom or context?
3. What tools and support will we need to be successful?

This logical progression allows our beliefs and practices to drive the acquisition of resources. Schools and districts become less susceptible to "*initiative du jour*" because they now have a set of steps and criteria in which to assess the possible effectiveness of the new tools. Teachers can also experience initiative fatigue if we constantly ask them to change up their habits without time to truly learn and use the technology.

One approach for starting small is engaging in a developmental pilot. Most educators are familiar with the pilot process, in which a small group of educators sign up to try out a resource or approach to instruction in their classrooms. They cover the ground rules for the pilot and agree to reconvene periodically to share their findings. The difference between a full pilot and a developmental pilot is that the developmental pilot has fewer expectations or strings attached. In my experience, the focus is on finding out what we don't know. No decisions are made in these engagements. It is about learning what works and what doesn't— and really exploring the technology to discover its possibilities. The freedom to play keeps the focus less on the tool and more on the process of learning itself.

In starting small, it might also be wise to create a table of contents for expected artifacts to upload into digital portfolios. This can give direction to a pilot without creating too many constraints. These artifacts can be related to one discipline, such as literacy. The focus can also be around a set of dispositions or values, such as service learning. Figure 5.1 is an example of an authentic writing portfolio table of contents. The digital tool would serve as the access point for housing students' writing and literacy-based projects. Student learning could travel from grade to grade. The purpose is specific to the discipline of writing; the audience might be other students and family members who could leave positive comments.

What the focus should be when starting small with digital portfolios is dependent on what the school is working toward as a community. In my prior school, we wanted to increase parent engagement. We used a dedicated portfolio application (FreshGrade) because of the ease with which families could receive notifications on their smartphones when a new artifact of learning was uploaded. In my new school, we might adopt a

Figure 5.1

Reading-Writing Portfolio Table of Contents

This document serves as a guide for students and teachers to build a portfolio of their work and authentically document their literacy skills. It is aligned with the Common Core State Standards. The goal is for students to present their portfolios at the spring conference (student-led conferences).

Introductory Letter
- ☐ Student biography; a description of their personal learning experience; summary of contents; importance of artifacts

Persuasive/Opinion Writing *(CCSS.ELA-LITERACY.CCRA.W.1)*
- ☐ Book review *(CCSS.ELA-LITERACY.CCRA.W.9)*
- ☐ Letter to the principal about a school issue
- ☐ Advertisement for a local business

Informative/Explanatory Writing *(CCSS.ELA-LITERACY.CCRA.W.2)*
- ☐ Research report *(CCSS.ELA-LITERACY.CCRA.W.7, CCSS.ELALITERACY.CCRA.W.8)*
- ☐ How-to essay
- ☐ Biography of historical figure or personal hero

Narrative/Imaginative Writing *(CCSS.ELA-LITERACY.CCRA.W.3)*
- ☐ Poetry
- ☐ Real narrative (e.g., small-moment writing, memoir)
- ☐ Fictional narrative

Process of Writing *(CCSS.ELA-LITERACY.CCRA.W.4, CCSS.ELA-LITERACY.CCRA.W.5)*
- ☐ Evidence of the different stages of the writing process (i.e., brainstorming, drafting, revising, editing, publishing)
- ☐ Evidence of ability to provide and accept feedback on writing

Digital Publishing *(CCSS.ELA-LITERACY.CCRA.W.6)*
- ☐ Blogging (e.g., slice of life, math journaling, science notebook)
- ☐ Digital storytelling (e.g., iMovie, YouTube)
- ☐ Multimedia creations (e.g., Little Bird Tales, Book Creator)

Range of Reading *(CCSS.ELA-LITERACY.CCRA.R.10)*
- ☐ List of books read including genre, rating, and review
- ☐ List of books on to-read list
- ☐ Reading conferences/fluency checks (audio recording)

Speaking and Listening *(CCSS.ELA-LITERACY.CCRA.SL.1, CCSS.ELALITERACY.CCRA.SL.4)*
☐ Podcasting (e.g., audioBoom, GarageBand)
☐ Storytelling
☐ Readers Theater
☐ Video tutorials (e.g., Educreations, Explain Everything)

Note on the reading-writing portfolio: Students would not be expected to include everything listed in this document every year. These ideas serve as suggestions for writing pieces, although book reviews and research reports do have anchor standards aligned with these activities. Each artifact should also be accompanied with a reflection. Consult your grade-level standards at www.corestandards.org for more information. This literacy assessment should travel with students from year to year. Students are expected to update their portfolios when they have produced a better piece or artifact. They should retain prior artifacts of learning to serve as evidence of growth over time. Primary students' reading-writing portfolios would be paper based with some digital artifacts posted for families to view periodically. Intermediate students would maintain a digital portfolio of their work over time. Digital portfolios would remain with students during their secondary career.

table of contents and use a digital tool that we feel best showcases student writing, such as Google Sites/Google Drive or Kidblog. If the pedagogy drives the decision making, then the choice regarding technology is more likely to be aligned with effective instruction and assessment. Starting small makes this messy process more manageable.

Attend to the Culture

The culture of a school relies heavily on the beliefs and actions the faculty exhibits in their instruction and collaboration. School leaders should consider how the introduction of digital portfolios entails more than just a change in resources. It is also a change in educators' practice. This type of change can be very personal and will require some attention.

One step to take when getting started is to revisit the school's mission and vision statements. Taking some time to unpack and discuss this language will remind everyone why they serve in schools. Leaders can also use this activity to segue into developing building norms, which are guidelines for how faculty members will conduct themselves when working with students and colleagues. They should be positively framed and general enough to apply to anyone. Examples include "Be prepared for teaching and learning," "Keep an open mind," and "Look for consensus on complex issues." Teachers and school leaders should come back to these norms when conversations about this change get heated.

When going schoolwide with digital portfolios, it is also helpful to tap into the emotional side of our role as educators. Leaders must attend to teachers' hearts as well as their minds. I have found that sharing a metaphor or a story is a great way to facilitate dialogue about better ways to assess student learning. For example, consider the message in the following Chinese folktale (Rodrigues, 2009):

> There was once an elderly Chinese woman who had two large pots, each hanging on the ends of a pole which she carried across her neck.
>
> One of the pots had a crack in it while the other pot was perfect and always delivered a full portion of water. At the end of the long walks from the stream to the house, the cracked pot arrived only half full.
>
> For a full two years this went on daily, with the woman bringing home only one and a half pots of water.
>
> Of course, the perfect pot was proud of its accomplishments. But the poor cracked pot was ashamed of its own imperfection and miserable that it could only do half of what it had been made to do.
>
> After two years of what it perceived to be bitter failure, it spoke to the woman one day by the stream: "I am ashamed of myself, because this crack in my side causes water to leak out all the way back to your house."

The old woman smiled, "Did you notice that there are flowers on your side of the path, but not on the other pot's side? That's because I have always known about your flaw, so I planted flower seeds on your side of the path, and every day while we walk back, you water them. For two years I have been able to pick these beautiful flowers to decorate the table. Without you being just the way you are, there would not be this beauty to grace the house."

Questions after the story can lead to deep discussions about the role of assessment in schools:

- How many of our students have been viewed through the lens of their deficiencies—of what they are not capable of instead of what's possible?
- What does a deficit approach do for a student's self-esteem? Their future?
- How can we address this situation with our assessments as a faculty?

Conversations such as this will more likely lead teachers to realize that they have some level of control over these circumstances. Staff might associate these types of stories with their students' own personal narratives, especially those with challenges and special needs. If this were my meeting, I might close out the discussion with the following to make the point clear: "Like the old woman, as teachers, we can create the conditions in which all of our students, regardless of their challenges, can succeed and even flourish as learners and as people. That's the rewarding part about teaching: designing the context for students to achieve and watching it happen. I believe portfolio assessment, with the help of digital tools, can make that happen."

Also consider the benefit of having protocols in place. Protocols are structures for facilitating professional conversations. In other words, rules and expectations are described ahead of time. The power of using protocols when attending to school culture is it provides a safer space for everyone to share their thinking—especially critical ideas. Most faculties tend to have a few more outspoken members. Although their ideas should be recognized, more reserved educators may have just as many beneficial things to share. In addition, protocols force people to listen when others are speaking. In my experience, people tend to wait to speak instead of actually hearing what someone else is saying. By using protocols, we maximize the potential that professional conversations can have on shifting a school culture in the right direction.

Recommended resources that contain useful protocols include *Data Wise: A Step-by-Step Guide to Using Assessment Results to Improving Teaching and Learning* (Boudett, City, & Murname, 2013) and *The Reflective Educator's Guide to Professional Development: Coaching Inquiry-Oriented Learning Communities* (Dana & Yendol-Hoppey, 2008).

Develop a Plan

Although culture is critical, clarity on the direction a school or district is taking is equally important. Developing an action plan helps create this clarity for staff, students, and families. (See Figure 5.2 for an example.) The plan should be created with a group of teacher leaders who will ensure that multiple perspectives are considered and honored. This document should explain what the initiative is; how it connects with the school's/ district's mission, vision, and current curriculum; benefits for students and the school; specific tools and resources needed for the work; a budget that considers software, hardware, and professional development; and a detailed timeline for implementation, including who is responsible for what and by when. Keeping the plan brief and visual in nature helps ensure that teachers will read and understand the details and purpose for implementing digital portfolios.

Figure 5.2

Digital Portfolios Action Plan

Grade/Discipline:

Team Members:

Prepared by:

Overview and Purpose:	Mission, Vision, and Curriculum Alignment:

	Anticipated Completion Date	Person(s) Responsible	
Rationale for digital portfolios (Identify benefits for students, staff, families; Select content/discipline focus)			Resources needed (software, hardware, professional development):
Initial implementation steps (Assign classrooms to pilot; Evaluate tool[s] and approach)			
Development of program (Create procedures; Specify content; Set standards)			Budget for resources:
Full implementation (Communicate plan; Provide training, time to implement)			
Regular portfolio evaluation (Convene leadership team to review and analyze portfolios)			Additional notes:

This action plan should be a work in progress. As unexpected situations arise, such as technical or technological challenges, there needs to be a way to adjust the timeline, tools, or approach to implementation. Just as important is aligning this technology initiative with the school's current curriculum and instruction. It is hard enough to make one change as an organization; trying to "fix" teaching with digital portfolios is not recommended. Instead, school leaders would be wise to approach this initiative with the goal of enhancing the high-quality practice already occurring in the school.

For example, if a school has experienced success in writing, then it might make sense to implement blogs as digital portfolios. This type of tool brings an authentic audience that might have been missing prior. Writing and blogging as a combination makes sense; this happens in the real world, especially with the posting and commenting features that tools such as Kidblog and Wordpress provide. The linked activity at the end of this chapter directs school leaders to the planning template in which they can create their own action plan based on the specific context of their building.

Offer Opportunities to Learn and Collaborate

Once a strong rationale for embedding digital portfolios and a plan for implementation have been established, leaders must allocate time and resources toward professional learning. Integrating technology at a deep level is a tall order for most teachers, regardless of their instructional ability.

To get everyone on the same page regarding digital portfolio assessment, it is essential to find time for basic training with the technology. I recommend creating and distributing an agenda ahead of time that requires teachers to come prepared (e.g., have apps downloaded and an account created). The agenda should also describe the goals for the initial training, who will be facilitating, and what roles everyone will play. With technology training for teachers, I also recommend having additional support on hand, such as technology staff and the teachers who initially piloted the initiative. They can walk around and assist teachers while the lead facilitator is demonstrating the tool.

It would be wise to expect some guidance and training from the technology provider itself. They are the experts on the product. Why not tap into their knowledge? In my prior school, we used Skype to video conference with a trainer to learn about FreshGrade, our tool of choice. She was the expert we did not have in house, aware of the ins and outs of the product plus the features that would be available soon. If a technology provider does not offer some type of support or training, then it's worth inquiring as to why, as well as where and how faculty could become fluent in using the digital tools.

After the initial whole-faculty training is complete, school leaders should develop a calendar of follow-up trainings and refreshers throughout the school year. Sharing these dates out ahead of time allows teachers to plan and make themselves available. Before each training session, send out a digital survey to solicit questions teachers might have about the digital portfolio tool. Their responses often serve as the agenda for the time together. Start by addressing these inquiries, and then provide time for teachers to use the technology and converse with one another. Feedback from these personalized training sessions can be collected through an online survey to improve future sessions.

Include Families in the Process

The home-school connection that can be facilitated with digital portfolios is essential. For many of our students, families will be their primary audience once they start sharing their best work and growth over time online. As already discussed, having an authentic audience for their work increases students' motivation to do their best. The feedback parents might leave on an online learning artifact also reinforces for teachers that they are paying attention to their children's work and care about their efforts. For some families who struggle to stay connected with their child's teacher and learning experiences, digital portfolios offer another pathway to facilitate communications. Relationships that are initially formed through online means can lead to developing a deeper connection with the school.

As a school looks into implementing digital portfolios en masse, it's wise to offer family members the opportunity to provide input into the process. This can take many forms. One approach is to invite families to after-school sessions to learn more about the technology. Some parents simply need to learn how to download the appropriate app or create login credentials. Once family members understand the basics, the educators facilitating the training can ask what they like and do not like about the tool and the school's approach to using it. This information can then be shared back with the faculty. Another idea is to create a digital survey and send it out to families via email or text message. Both approaches involve families in the process, which can increase ownership in any decision to move forward with the technology and assessment initiative.

Another reason to include families in the process of implementing digital portfolios is because they might bring additional resources to your efforts. The most obvious benefit is the funds that a parent group could raise to support hardware purchases or software subscriptions. If financial support is not an issue, some parents or family members might have a background in technology. Consider tapping them for advice or even as technology support. Family members can also provide insights about what they would prefer to see posted in their children's digital portfolios and how often.

One final benefit to allowing families to be a part of the implementation process is the community support that will naturally develop. Many parents are still nervous about allowing their child to be online. They have reasonable anxieties. This may cause some conflict if a few family members try to resist the initiative. If, however, there are enough families who believe that student learning artifacts should not be sequestered to the school, they can become your greatest area of support. I have found that parents and other family members carry much more political clout than I or any other educator might have with district leadership. They can be integral in getting this type of change to move forward. Making families our allies from an educational, financial, and political stance will help ensure this initiative is successful.

Be Willing to Pay

The idea that some technologies are "free" still perpetuates the educational dialogue, especially online. The fact is, nothing is free. Even if there is no cost to the school to use certain software, the companies that develop it might use student information and data for their own purposes. For example, one of Google's biggest revenue producers is the advertising they sell within their search engine and related applications. Our search inquiries and the websites with which we engage provide information for Google to tailor what we see in terms of ads and pop ups. Even through Google's G Suite for Education—which is not supposed to use student information to sell advertising—we're immersing students in a product the developer certainly hopes kids will continue using in the future.

I am not suggesting that schools avoid accessing Google or any other digital tool that is "free" to use. But I do believe that we need to understand—and help students understand—that we do pay in some form or fashion when we use these tools and technologies. Another concern regarding the use of "free" digital tools is that only the largest companies can actually afford to offer this policy. This means that schools might overlook software or hardware that could possibly lead to better outcomes in student learning. Related, smaller technology companies are typically focused on doing one or two things really well. For example, Kidblog is about one thing: blogging. Within their ecosystem, teachers can connect with other classrooms also using Kidbog, set preferred privacy levels, and know that student data are most likely being maintained with integrity. I also find that smaller technology companies typically provide better customer support.

When it's time to move forward from a technology pilot to the adoption of a schoolwide solution or tool, it's a good idea to talk with a company sales representative first. Consider the following questions:

- Where do you store your data? Where are the servers located? (security)
- How long would we be under contract for your service? (transparency)
- What type of support will you provide for teachers when they need help? (customer service)
- Who "owns" the data? Does student information belong to students and their families? (rights)
- How is your company funded: by subscriptions or through investments? If you rely on investors, what are their origins? (integrity)

If the representative is able to answer these questions— or similar ones—without a lot of dancing around or avoidance, then chances are good that the technology provider has developed the digital portfolio tool for the right reason: to improve student learning outcomes.

Summary

As previously stated, there is more than one pathway a school leader can take in implementing digital portfolios at a schoolwide level. Every school has a different culture and climate. Having completed this type of change before and becoming more familiar with the literature and research on organizational change, I am confident that school leaders who follow these general steps will likely experience success.

- Start with assessments. This includes expanding the types of assessments being used and developing assessment literacy with faculty.
- Assess your level of readiness. Without available and robust technologies—both hardware and software—we risk running any digital initiative into the ground.
- Start small. Instead of pushing every teacher to adopt digital portfolios, allow faculty who are ready for this initiative to run a pilot.
- Attend to the culture. Introducing digital assessments into instruction is a cultural change as well as a technical change. Teachers need to believe in the importance of this type of work.
- Develop a plan. Create a committee of interested staff (and even students) to develop a process, timeline, and formal action plan for implementing digital portfolios schoolwide.
- Offer opportunities to learn and collaborate. As school leaders, we are only one person. Let others facilitate the professional development and training whenever possible.
- Include families in the process. Parents and students have insights that are essential as a school moves forward with technology integration. They will become your champions for change if you let them have a voice in the process.
- Be willing to pay. There is no such thing as "free" technology. Do your homework about the technology company you are interested in and allocate funds on a yearly basis for these resources as needed.

Above all, enjoy the journey in upgrading your assessment practices with the help of digital tools. Learning should be an exciting and rewarding experience for everyone involved in the process.

Linked Activity: Develop an Action Plan for Digital Portfolios

Use the templates provided in this chapter to assess your school's readiness and start creating a plan for implementing digital portfolios schoolwide. Use online collaborative software and share out this process with all stakeholders to ensure transparency and garner feedback. Make sure this work is tightly aligned with the school's mission, vision, beliefs, and values to ensure that pedagogy is driving the effort. Take this process as slowly as it needs to go. With digital portfolios, and technology integration in general, doing it well is better than getting it done.

Learner Profile: Josh Beck and Chris Haeger

Josh Beck is a high school English teacher at Cudahy High School in Cudahy, Wisconsin, not far from Milwaukee. Chris Haeger is the building principal. Josh and Chris share their journey in adopting a more authentic and continuous approach to student assessment with digital tools.

Q&A Why did you introduce digital portfolio assessment in your classroom?

Chris: Our focus was on developing a growth-minded assessment with kids, following the research available that supports this work. We wanted to move beyond just a grade—to give kids an opportunity to see their growth over time. The advent of the Common Core State Standards helped in providing us with direction.

Josh: As teachers, we knew the standards were coming. We wanted to authentically assess students' understanding of those standards and to measure our impact as educators. We decided that portfolios were a way to do this. It's great how students can go back and see how they grew from semester to semester. As teachers, we could see how we have influenced our students' work in literacy.

In what way(s) were the effects of implementing digital portfolios in school unique or unusual?

Chris: Twice a year, sophomores and seniors present their portfolios to a panel of adults. Businesspeople, community leaders, college professors, members of the military, and members of our state's department of public instruction have all served on this board. This experience has been tremendously positive. Students have to come in front of all these people and present what they have learned and done and tell us how their work has displayed their understanding. Putting themselves out there, wearing suits and dresses, is a great experience for them. Kids will come back and tell us how this experience is tangibly dependent on the academic expectations.

Josh: One student did not come prepared to the panel. She had to explain to everyone why she did not do any work that semester. The next time, she was dressed up and had work to present that addressed all 10 ELA standards. The portfolio process was what motivated her to move out of a fixed mindset due to her situation. Now I just ask the kids, "What are you going to present at the panel?" These experiences also lead to real opportunities. After one presentation, a student was asked by a local employer if she wanted to apply for a position.

How would you describe the characteristics of the products from the digital portfolio work and of the educators who were involved?

Josh: Other content areas and departments have joined us in this process. We put together a list of the standards in plain

English, shared them with the other teachers, and asked, "What assignments are aligned with these expectations?" We have sat down with social studies teachers, government teachers, and talked about the work they do with kids and how they might connect with one another. For example, when students study the U.S. Constitution and we read *The Kite Runner,* we compare the different constitutions between Afghanistan and the United States, especially after 9/11 and how our country was involved. Conversations about how to include minorities and females in our own county's constitution are more frequent and deep.

What resources were used to support the use of digital portfolios?

Chris: We use Chromebooks to access many of these resources. High school students all have one of these devices. Also, it was critical that there was teacher willingness to move from binders on a shelf to something electronically based. Our technology integration specialist was able to help teachers support this initiative and solve any glitches. He has been instrumental. Kids all now have a Google Site that maintains their portfolios.

Josh: After they graduate, students will come back and connect their personal emails to keep those portfolios. One student who went to college used her high school template to develop another one for her English coursework. The panelists have also liked this digital component. The ability to quickly click on a link and show four years' worth of work is very convenient.

What specific outcomes do you attribute to the use of digital portfolios?

Chris: It has expanded kids' understanding of technology. We have shown them how to use their phones beyond social media and texting. Even teaching kids how to create a website is important. We aren't making any assumptions about kids' "tech-savvyness." Kids who transfer into our district are amazed at how technology is used and how applicable basic tools are, such as smartphones and copy machines. We are using all tools to allow students to learn. Other apps, such as voice recorders and video makers, are incorporated into their Google Site.

In your opinion, what other factors contributed to the achievement of these outcomes?

Josh: Again, the willingness of the staff is impressive. We are trying to connect with kids on a personal level—to be reflective and develop relationships. We talk about what they did well and what they want to work on next. We are constantly asking the kids for feedback and asking how our instruction helped them meet expectations. An added benefit has been how we have taught students to network and reach out to others to include them in the panel and process.

Chris: Also, the willingness of community members to come in and listen to the kids describe their learning is nice. The kids see the mayor here, other important leaders, and they take what is really their final exam, and it creates a different context. At least half of our kids show up in suits and ties. People are now calling us to serve on this panel and have taken an interest in the students' learning. Another factor is panelists have told us it is easier to answer educational questions and have conversations with people about this topic in the community. The indirect influence of this process has brought in other leaders to our school.

What problems did you encounter when developing or introducing digital portfolios?

Chris: Students tell us that the first time through is a learning process regarding organization. Kids talk and discuss how different teachers have different expectations regarding the portfolios. Also, staff members needed some time to adjust. "How is the portfolio connected to standards? Learning targets?" Portfolios point out many more areas of school that need to be addressed.

Josh: It was a slow process in the beginning because the seniors didn't have a digital portfolio. So we had to transition. It was also a challenge to get everyone on the same page regarding academic expectations and how the standards are interpreted. What is acceptable and what is not, and defining what these standards are asking for—we as a faculty have to have a common understanding. Parents are involved in this process up to the presentation itself, preparing them for the event.

What else do you think a teacher or school should know before implementing digital portfolios?

Josh: The presentation is a celebration of their work. They come to the end of the school year with excitement and pride, smiles on their faces. "When do you present?" and "How did you do?" are common questions we hear in the hallways. Even students with significant needs are expected to present. The panelists can never tell which kids are in a special education program and which are not. One student who is autistic came up and delivered an amazing presentation without any echoing or other issues that he normally displays. We were so glad to have given him the opportunity to do this on his own and be independent. Everyone talked about it afterward from the panel. Successes like this—kids coming in like any other kid—it is amazing.

Moving Beyond
Digital Portfolios

"Uncertainty is the foundation for inquiry and research."

—Peter Johnston

A family friend, Lisl H. Detlefsen, is a children's book author. She has been persistent in her efforts to get to this point in her career. She received multiple rejections before publishers started saying *yes* to her work. I asked her if she kept a portfolio that was representative of her growth as a writer in addition to one that showed her best work. I assumed professional writers kept a collection of these artifacts to share and promote when pitching their next idea. Her response was surprising: "No, I work with an agent. When I have a new manuscript ready for submission, she knows which editors are most likely to be interested in it."

She does have a website that highlights her publications, readers' positive reviews, and upcoming events she is hosting (www.lislhdbooks.com). However, this web presence is a small part of how she represents herself as an artist to the larger world. The connections she has with editors, her agent, and other writers are more important than any digital presence she might have. It is about who she knows as much as who knows her and what she can do. These collaborators help bring her a broader audience and offer her helpful guidance to become better in her work. Without these relationships—mediated both online and offline—she might still be trying to get her first book published.

This example illustrates an important point about digital portfolios. In the real world, they don't exist—at least, not as the formalized constructs educators create for classroom use. My writer friend does not publish a new piece of writing or art every six weeks and add reflective comments to it. Lisl does not have a teacher who checks in with her regularly to assess her progress and offer feedback and ideas for future goals. Yes, she does work with editors and mentors to improve her practice, and she does post highlights on her site, such as when her next book will be coming out. But it is her work that drives her presence, not the other way around. Also important is that what she produces is her own. Her website merely houses her work; she can take her content with her whenever the need arises.

In this brief chapter, we'll take a closer look at the importance of all learners claiming their own digital domains during their K–12 careers. In addition, we'll explore three areas—gradeless classrooms, self-publishing, and Genius Hour—as possible next steps in helping our students truly own their learning both today, tomorrow, and for the foreseeable future.

Claiming Our Domain

We have to take the long view when it comes to facilitating portfolio assessment with digital tools. These are often not spaces that students can take with them once their K–12 careers are complete. With this in mind, what is the larger aim of this venture? What type of learning experiences can we facilitate on behalf of our students that will last for a lifetime?

Audrey Watters (2016) takes up this issue in her work regarding modern learning. She poses several questions regarding ownership of student learning and the content that has been created and documented. "What happens now that schoolwork is increasingly digital (that is, schoolwork that isn't paperwork but has been digitized as done directly on computers)? Schoolwork done on computers should prompt other questions too, such as: What counts as student work? Content? Data? What happens to that work, not just at the end of the school year but on a day-to-day basis?" (p. 2)

Data collection has become a high priority in schools. The question is: How might we define *data* today, especially as the traditional understanding continues to broaden with the abundance of new technologies accessible in schools? Audio, video, and images are all potential artifacts that can inform learning and teaching. However, the ephemeral nature of digital content, at least what we can see in front of us, demands a different approach to how we collect, curate, and share our work. "We must consider what student data are being created, what student data are being collected (and by whom), how to protect that data, and how to preserve it. Furthermore, we must put the control of that data into the hands of the students themselves, in no small part because learning now happens beyond school walls (and school software)—at home and on the go, thanks to mobile devices" (Watters, 2016, p. 4). This is an issue of both student safety and learning legacy.

With this in mind, what is possible for our students today and in the near future? I believe that it's critical for students to be able to take control of their learning histories. Let's look at three opportunities to do just that.

The Gradeless Classroom

In my experience, once teachers start utilizing digital portfolios to communicate student learning on a regular basis, one of the first school constructs they question is grading. As a former teacher asked me, "If I'm sharing their work online and then parents can see how they are doing, why is grading necessary?" This is a hard question to answer. We should not drop grades on a whim, yet we cannot deny the power of digital portfolios as a more effective assessment tool for documenting student progress and achievement (at least when implemented with fidelity).

Mark Barnes outlines an alternative approach to responding to and assessing student learning using feedback as the primary source of communication. He uses the acronym SE2R as a mnemonic device for remembering how to respond to work submitted from student to teacher (Barnes, 2013). It stands for

- Summarize
- Explain
- Redirect
- Resubmit

Using this systematic approach to feedback, teachers can be more consistent in their assessment practices and possibly stop the practice of formal/traditional grading. "The days of placing a number or a letter at the top of a student's paper and blotting red ink all over the margins must come to an end if education is to move into the 21st century and beyond" (Barnes, 2013, p. 87). If the feedback is consistent, timely, specific, and moves learners forward, there is little reason why an approach like this could not be a better alternative to the somewhat arbitrary symbols and numbers that have represented student learning in the past. The absence of grades does not mean the absence of student ownership. By not associating a grade with student work, we may improve the feeling of authorship with the student, assuming the work is authentic and meaningful.

Barnes also offers some insights into his thinking as he works with a student:

> I begin by telling students what they've done. This may sound inconsequential, but many students complete tasks aim-

lessly and never realize what they've actually accomplished. Further explanation of what was done and how it does or doesn't meet learning outcomes or follow a specific set of guidelines is critical to the learning process. If something is missed, students are redirected to a specific lesson, presentation, or model so learning can be reemphasized. Sometimes, redirection can be as simple as "see me for clarification." When redirection is given, students are always asked to resubmit the activity or project for further evaluation. (Barnes, 2013, pp. 75–76)

As already discussed, high-quality feedback is a pillar of effectively utilizing formative assessment. The inclusion of digital tools such as progress and process portfolios can facilitate this approach. The comments and revisions that result from feedback offered by the teacher can be captured and shared within a portfolio platform. This information can serve as the necessary evidence to gauge whether students have met the expectations for learning and how deeply. When a family member is included in the learning trajectory on a regular basis, the need for grades and other arbitrary symbols is lessened. Instead, the process becomes simply about the learning.

A reality with gradeless classrooms is how graduation works once students meet all of the necessary credit requirements in high school. Some private high schools have addressed this situation by moving toward competency-based education. Many of the private high schools participating in this innovation to "embrace a new transcript" are attempting to measure proficiency in what leaders believe are key areas for students' future success, including "Complex Communication—Oral and Written" and "Integrity and Ethical Decision Making" (Jaschik, 2017). The model envisions that each credit earned would be backed up by examples of student work, so an admissions officer could see lab reports, essays, and so forth. Students curate their examples of work in "digital lockers"—another term for portfolios.

Student Self-Publishing

It is reasonable to expect students to internalize the qualities and criteria for what good work looks like in any given subject or discipline. This is an essential step in guiding students to become independent, self-directed learners. When someone knows what success looks like and they have the tools to guide themselves toward that end goal, they can learn almost anything they set their mind to.

One of the best opportunities for students to showcase their learning in an authentic way is through self-publishing. The concept of self-publishing itself is not necessarily new. If a prospective author struggled to get a manuscript accepted, he or she would seek out independent opportunities to get the work in front of an audience. Yet even these opportunities can be fleeting. A printing press had to be willing to take on the project, and the author had to be willing to take a financial loss if not enough people were to purchase the book. There was big risk with little assurance of reward.

In today's digital world, however, the prospect of self-publishing has become a greater reality for any author-to-be, adult or student. One example of a digital self-publishing tool is CreateSpace (www.createspace.com). With CreateSpace, writers can upload their manuscripts, design covers, assign ISBN numbers, and review proofs to ensure accuracy of the text. Once everything looks ready, the final draft is uploaded and posted online for anyone to purchase. The price of each book is set based on what the author believes is reasonable. The final product can be available for digital e-readers and in print.

Students have the opportunity not only to produce a real book but also to tangle with the details of sales, marketing, and profit sharing. Self-publishing becomes an opportunity for integrating literacy with economics. Students are no longer developing a digital portfolio but rather a digital presence that can give them credibility for years to come. Another option, especially for younger students, is to use Book Creator to create original ebooks with embedded audio. This work can be published to YouTube or iBooks.

Genius Hour

Helping students own their learning should not be reserved for the content they produce. Ownership is also about how students choose to spend their time at school, even if for a little bit.

Genius Hour, which is sometimes referred to as 20 percent time, has become more prevalent in education today. Google started this concept when they gave their employees the equivalent of one day a week to work on their passion projects. What they worked on must be related to their mission as a company, but the specifics were entirely up to them. Some of their best ideas, such as the concept of collaborative writing via Google Docs, came out of this concept of 20 percent time.

National surveys continue to show that the longer students spend in school, the less engaged they feel with learning in general (Busteed, 2013). This should be cause for alarm, yet we still deal almost exclusively with expected outcomes and meeting standards in the name of ensuring every student is successful. But successful at what? Are these successes on students' own terms? Genius Hour is one way teachers and schools devote time for student choice and voice.

This can look different in every school. Some teachers have incorporated Genius Hour, in which kids are provided time, space, and resources to explore their interests and passions in a guided inquiry-based approach to learning. The authors of *The Genius Hour Handbook: Fostering Passion, Wonder, and Inquiry in the Classroom* (Krebs & Zvi, 2016) highlight many benefits for students when effectively implementing Genius Hour in classrooms:

- They have autonomy and purpose.
- They are given time to master content.
- They make good learning decisions.

- They become fearless learners.
- They can stop playing the game of getting good grades.
- They develop curiosity, innovation, and creativity.
- They explore and wonder to discover their passions.
- They will be better understood by teacher and peers.
- They will be instructional leaders as they share their projects.

My wife, a former 2nd grade teacher, tried this out in her classroom of very active students. She facilitated Genius Hour, which her students referred to as "project time," at the end of the day. This was a time in which students could tinker and make things of their choosing. Resources such as building kits and creative art materials were provided with little direction. What she found was that choice affected each student in different ways. Some students liked working with peers regularly, whereas others needed quiet time to read and write. For one student in particular, a half hour of tinkering every day led to a reduction in office referrals by 70 percent. Providing choice in school helped her better understand her students and adjust her instruction.

The challenge with concepts such as Genius Hour—which allow for more student choice and voice—is how to document learning. For my wife, the answer came with the use of digital portfolios. Instead of instituting one specific type of portfolio, she captured students' best work as well as the processes they used to achieve their goals. This process brought an authentic audience for students' real work, and students felt like their ideas were validated through the use of digital tools to capture and celebrate their efforts.

Conclusion: Rethinking Assessment in the 21st Century

What the future holds for teaching and learning is hard to predict. Will all textbooks go digital, or will they even cease to exist? How will technology improve in its ability to provide feedback for student learning as it happens and then adjust accordingly? What role will students' interests and goals play in their educational experiences? What is yet to come is both exciting and a cause for anxiety.

One area in which I feel comfortable making a prediction is how assessment will change. Really, it already has. Schools and districts are going gradeless. Learning management systems are putting students in the driver's seat regarding growth and achievement. Parents can see how their children are doing in school at any given moment without the arbitrariness of grades and scores. As these practices become more widespread, the expectations for all schools will shift in this direction.

Digital portfolios are a way for teachers to explore a better approach to assessment in the 21st century. They celebrate student work in a visible way. Technology integration with a clear purpose helps students and teachers manage the multiple streams of information flowing in the classroom. The audiences that digital portfolio assessment can facilitate—both locally and globally—can be a main driver for students to produce their best work. Access to the relevant and appropriate tools become more available every day.

By understanding and acting upon the belief that students can lead their own learning, we realize true success as educators. Digital portfolio assessment, from celebrating best work to measuring growth over time and eventually to students calling their digital presence their own, is one approach to this destination.

If you would like to continue this conversation, share your work, and interact with other educators who are also pursuing digital portfolios, then please join our vibrant Google+ community: http://bit.ly/dspinaction. This approach to assessment in the 21st century is just the beginning. Let's come together and learn how to leverage technology in a way that honors the whole child.

Appendix A: Digital Portfolio Assessment Readiness Tool

Directions: Rate your classroom/school/district on each component for these domains. Celebrate where you are accomplished, and consider how to move forward in other areas.

Access	Accomplished	Getting There	Not Started
Availability (How many tools do students have available to connect with?)			
Connectivity (What is the strength and breadth of your school's wireless system?)			
Compatibility (Are the selected tools compatible with the needs of the learners?)			
Allocation (Is there adequate time, funding, and training devoted to learning about and using these tools?)			

Purpose	Accomplished	Getting There	Not Started
Resources (What is the rationale for using the selected technology, both hardware and software?)			
Content (How is technology connected to essential questions and understandings?)			
Integration (Will embedding technology into your curriculum, instruction, and assessment augment learning?)			
Agency (Do learners have the opportunity to self-assess and improve upon their work, and thereby perceive that their additional effort increases their ability?)			

Audience	Accomplished	Getting There	Not Started
Visibility (Is the learning students produce shareable with a broader audience?)			
Independence (Does an audience motivate students to self-assess their own work and produce learning aligned with their potential?)			
Inquiry (Will new knowledge and skills lead to new questions and investigations?)			
Empathy (Can students broaden their horizons by actively listening to others, engaging in conversations, and providing feedback in the classroom and beyond?)			

Appendix B:
Planning Template for Digital
Portfolios in the Classroom

Step 1: Determine the planning time and discipline for a yearlong plan for instruction.

When will we meet to prepare for next year?

What discipline will we focus on in our planning?

How will we know that we are successful?

Step 2: Bring in assessment data, including samples of student work, to identify strengths and areas for growth within the discipline of focus.

Strengths	Areas for Growth
•	•
•	•
•	•

Step 3: Determine a digital portfolio tool with which to post student work.

- Choice A: Blogs (e.g., Kidblog, Edublogs, Wordpress, Blogger)
- Choice B: Dedicated Portfolio Applications (e.g., FreshGrade, Seesaw)
- Choice C: Websites (e.g., Google Sites, Weebly)

Step 4: Schedule publishing dates on which performance tasks will be uploaded to students' digital portfolios, accompanied with reflections, self-assessment, and goal setting.

Publishing Date:	Unit:
Publishing Date:	Unit:
Publishing Date:	Unit:
Publishing Date:	Unit:
Publishing Date:	Unit:
Publishing Date:	Unit:
Publishing Date:	Unit:

References

Allington, R. L., & Cunningham, P. M. (2006). *Schools that work: Where all children read and write* (2nd ed.). Boston: Allyn & Bacon.

Barnes, M. (2013). *Role reversal: Achieving uncommonly excellent results in the student-centered classroom.* Alexandria, VA: ASCD.

Barshay, J. (2016). Using computers widens the achievement gap in writing, a federal study finds. *The Hechinger Report.* Available: http://hechinger report.org/online-writing-tests-widen-achievement-gap

Black, P., & Wiliam, D. (1998). Inside the black box: Raising standards through classroom assessment. *Phi Delta Kappan, 80*(2), 139–144, 146–148.

Boudett, K. P., City, E. A., & Murname, R. J. (2013). *Data wise: A step-by-step guide to using assessment results to improving teaching and learning* (2nd ed.). Cambridge, MA: Harvard Education Press.

Boushey, G., & Moser, J. (2014). *The daily 5: Fostering literacy independence in the elementary grades* (2nd ed.). Portland, ME: Stenhouse.

Busteed, B. (2013). The school cliff: Student engagement drops with each school year. Available: www.gallup.com/opinion/gallup/170525/school-cli-student-engagement-drops-school-year.aspx

Dana, N. F., & Yendol-Hoppey, D. (2008). *The reflective educator's guide to professional development: Coaching inquiry-oriented learning communities.* Thousand Oaks, CA: Corwin.

Davidson, K. (2016). These are the "soft skills" employers are looking for. *The Wall Street Journal.* Available: http://blogs.wsj.com/economics/2016/08/30/the-soft-skills-employers-are-looking-for

Evans, C. S. (1993). When teachers look at student work. *Educational Leadership, 50*(5), 71–72.

Institute for Habits of Mind. (n.d.) About us. Retrieved May 18, 2017, from www.habitsofmindinstitute.org/about-us/us

International Society for Technology in Education. (2017). ISTE standards for students. Retrieved May 18, 2017, from www.iste.org/standards/standards/for-students

Isaacson, W. (2011). *Steve Jobs.* New York: Simon & Schuster.

Jaschik, S. (2017). A plan to kill high school transcripts . . . and transform college admissions. *Inside Higher Ed.* Available: www.insidehighered.com/news/2017/05/10/top-private-high-schools-start-campaign-kill-traditional-transcripts-and-change

Jenkins, C. B. (1996). *Inside the writing portfolio: What we need to know to assess children's writing.* Portsmouth, NH: Heinemann.

Johnston, P. H. (2012). *Opening minds: Using language to change lives.* Portland, ME: Stenhouse.

Krebs, D., & Zvi, G. (2016). *The genius hour guidebook: Fostering passion, wondering, and inquiry in the classroom.* New York: Routledge.

Larmer, J., Mergendoller, J., & Boss, S. (2015). *Setting the standard for project based learning: A proven approach to rigorous classroom instruction.* Alexandria, VA: ASCD.

Marinak, B. A., Malloy, J. B., Gambrell, L. B., & Mazzoni, S. A. (2015). Me and my reading profile: A tool for assessing early reading motivation. *The Reading Teacher, 69*(1), 51–62.

Moore, E. (2015). Planning for the planning [blog post]. Retrieved from *Two Writing Teachers* at https://twowritingteachers.org/2015/05/11/planning-for-june-planning

Moss, C. M., & Brookhart, S. M. (2012). *Learning targets: Helping students aim for understanding in today's lesson.* Alexandria, VA: ASCD.

Moya, S. S., & O'Malley, J. M. (1994). A portfolio assessment model for ESL. *The Journal of Educational Issues of Language Minority Students, 13,* 13–36.

Niguidula, D. (2010). Digital portfolios and curriculum maps: Linking teacher and student work. In H. H. Jacobs (Ed.), *Curriculum 21: Essential education for a changing world.* Alexandria, VA: ASCD.

November, A. (2012). *Who owns the learning? Preparing students for success in the digital age.* Bloomington, IN: Solution Tree.

Palmer, E. (2014). Now presenting . . . *Educational Leadership. 72*(3), 24–29.

Perkins, D. (2014). *Future wise: Educating our children for a changing world.* San Francisco, CA: Jossey-Bass.

Popham, W. J. (2008). *Transformative assessment.* Alexandria, VA: ASCD.

Reeves, A. R. (2011). *Where great teaching begins: Planning for student thinking and learning.* Alexandria, VA: ASCD.

Renwick, M. (2014). *Digital student portfolios: A whole school approach to connected learning and continuous assessment.* Virginia Beach, VA: Powerful Learning Press.

Renwick, M. (2015). *5 myths about classroom technology: How can we integrate digital tools to truly enhance learning?* Alexandria, VA: ASCD.

Renwick, M. (2016). Initial findings after implementing digital student portfolios in elementary classrooms [blog post]. Retrieved from *Reading by Example* at https://readingbyexample.com/2016/06/27/initial-findings-after-implementing-digital-student-portfolios-in-elementary-classrooms

Rodrigues, D. (2009). The cracked pot. Retrieved from www.barry4kids.net

Routman, R. (in press). *Literacy essentials: Engagement, excellence, and equity for ALL learners.* Portsmouth, NH: Stenhouse.

Sagor, R.D. (2010). *The action research guidebook: A four-stage process for educators and school teams.* Thousand Oaks, CA: Corwin.

Spencer, J. (2016). *Launch: Using design thinking to boost creativity and bring out the maker in every student.* San Diego, CA: Dave Burgess Consulting.

Stefanakis, E.H. (2002). *Multiple intelligences and portfolios: A window into the learner's mind.* Portsmouth, NH: Heinemann.

Tovani, C. (2010). *So what do they really know? Assessment that informs teaching and learning.* Portsmouth, NH: Stenhouse.

Toyoma, K. (2015). Why technology alone won't fix schools. *The Atlantic.* Retrieved from www.theatlantic.com/education/archive/2015/06/why-technology-alone-wont-fix-schools/394727

Valencia, S.W., & Place, N. (1994). Literacy portfolios for teaching, learning, and accountability: The Bellevue Literacy Assessment Project. *Authentic Reading Assessment: Practices and Possibilities, 134–156.*

Watters, A. (2016). *Claim your domain—and own your online presence.* Bloomington, IN: Solution Tree.

Wiggins, G., & McTighe, J. (2005). *Understanding by design* (expanded 2nd ed.). Alexandria, VA: ASCD.

Wiliam, D. (2011). *Embedded formative assessment.* Bloomington, IN: Solution Tree.

Index

The letter *f* following a page number denotes a figure.

About the Author

 **Matt Renwick** is an elementary principal in Mineral Point, Wisconsin. He is married to Jodi and the father of Finn and Violet. Prior to this position, Matt was a teacher and school administrator in Wisconsin Rapids. He is the author of *Digital Student Portfolios: A Whole School Approach to Connected Learning and Continuous Assessment* (2014) and the ASCD Arias book *5 Myths About Classroom Technology: How Do We Integrate Digital Tools to Truly Enhance Learning?* (2015). Matt posts frequently on his collaborative blog for literacy leaders, Reading by Example (www.readingbyexample.com), and tweets at @ReadByExample. He also writes for Discovery Education and Lead Literacy. For more information about Matt's work, go to his website, www.mattrenwick.com.

Related ASCD Resources

At the time of publication, the following ASCD resources were available (ASCD stock numbers in parentheses). For up-to-date information about ASCD resources, go to www.ascd.org. Search the complete archives of *Educational Leadership* at www.ascd.org/el.

ASCD EDge®

Exchange ideas and connect with other educators on the social networking site ASCD EDge at http://ascdedge.ascd.org.

ASCD myTeachSource®

Download resources from a professional learning platform with hundreds of research-based best practices and tools for your classroom at http://myteachsource.ascd.org/.

Print Products

Advancing Formative Assessment in Every Classroom: A Guide for Instructional Leaders by Connie M. Moss and Susan M. Brookhart (#109031)

Checking for Understanding: Formative Assessment Techniques for Your Classroom, 2nd ed., by Douglas Fisher and Nancy Frey (#115011)

Five Myths About Classroom Technology: How do we integrate digital tools to truly enhance learning? (ASCD Arias) by Matt Renwick (#SF115069)

Grading Smarter, Not Harder: Assessment Strategies That Motivate Kids and Help Them Learn by Myron Dueck (#114003)

Great Performances: Creating Classroom-Based Assessment Tasks, 2nd ed., by Larry Lewin and Betty Jean Shoemaker (#110038)

Peer Feedback in the Classroom: Empowering Students to Be the Experts by Starr Sackstein (#117020)

For more information: send e-mail to member@ascd.org; call 1-800-933-2723 or 703-578-9600, press 2; send a fax to 703-575-5400; or write to Information Services, ASCD, 1703 N. Beauregard St., Alexandria, VA 22311-1714 USA.